AMC 10 12 고득점을 위한 필독서

심선생의
AMC10 AMC12 만점정복

심현성 지음

본 책은 SAT, AP 전문 사이트인 마스터프렙(www.masterprep.net)의 동영상 강의 교재로 제작이 되었으므로 해설은 제공되지 않습니다. 본 책에 대한 심현성 선생님의 저자직강 해설 강의는 마스터프렙에서만 보실 수 있습니다.

저자
소개

심현성(Albert Shim) 선생님은

  수능수학과 경시수학을 가르치다가 미국수학 전문가가 되었다. 레카스 아카데미를 거쳐 블루키프렙 대표이사 겸 대표강사를 지내다가 현재 TOP SEM학원의 대표이사 겸 Math 대표강사이기도 하다. 2008년 한국에서는 처음으로 "Math Level 2"를 출간 하였고 연이어 2009년에는 처음으로 "AP calculus"출간하였다. 현재는 10개국 이상의 나라에 Math관련 교재를 출간하고 있다. 특히, "Math Level 2 10 Practice Tests" , "AP Calculus AB&BC 핵심 편", "AP Calculus AB&BC 심화 편", "AMC10 & 12 특강"등은 미국 대학을 준비하는 거의 모든 학생들의 필수서적이 될 만큼 중요한 교재이며 베스트셀러 교재이기도 하다.

  2008년부터 지금까지 10개국 이상에 출간한 책이 20권 이상이며 압구정에서 가장 많은 수강생을 가르치는 유명강사이다. 오프라인에서는 압구정에 위치한 TOP SEM학원에서 강의하고 있으며 온라인에서는 SAT,AP,IB 즉 미국대학 입시 전문 인터넷 동영상 강의 전문업체인 마스터프렙(www.masterprep.net)에서 Math의 거의 모든 분야를 강의하고 있으며 해당 사이트에서도 No.1 수학강사로 차별성 있는 톡톡 뛰는 강의로 정평이 나 있다.

수업문의

TOP SEM학원 (02-511-4235, www.topsem.co.kr)
인터넷 동영상업체 마스터프렙 (www.masterprep.net)

 # 책의 특징과 효과적인 공부법

1. 각 단원별로 기본적인 문제부터 고난이도 문제까지 골고루 실려 있다.
2. 기본적인 문제라고 해서 그냥 지나치지 말자. 모든 고난이도 문제는 기본적인 문제에서 시작을 한다. 기본적인 문제의 정확한 풀이를 이해해야 고난이도 문제가 해결이 된다.
3. 모든 문제들을 여러 번 반복해서 풀어봐야 한다. 문제 번호와 페이지가 외워질 정도로 반복을 하여야 한다.
4. AMC10과 AMC12는 많은 단원들이 일치한다. AMC12의 경우 몇몇 단원들이 추가가 되는데 AMC10에 응시하려는 학생들도 되도록 AMC12까지 공부하는 것이 좋다.
5. 각 단원의 문제배열은 난이도 순이 아니다. 대부분의 단원들이 처음에는 기본적인 문제들로 시작을 하지만 중간 중간에 고난이도 문제들도 배치를 하였다.
6. 모든 문제를 한 번에 풀려고 하지말자. 시간을 두고 조금씩 꾸준히 풀어나간다.
7. 어느 단원은 개념을 연습시키기 위한 문제들(Exercise)을 실었다. 이 문제들도 몇 번이고 반복해서 풀어봐야 한다. AMC고난이도 문제와 AIME문제들을 해결하는데 필요한 개념을 담은 문제들이기 때문이다.

AMC 시험에 대해서···

응시제한과 채점은 다음과 같다.

AMC10	10학년(17.5세)이하	25문항 객관식/75분	각6점/150점 만점 Blank Answer 1.5
AMC12	12학년(19.5세)이하	25문항 객관식/75분	각6점/150점 만점 Blank Answer 1.5

AMC10의 경우 상위 2.5%이상이거나 120점 이상 AMC12의 경우 상위 5%이상이거나 100점 이상이면 AIME응시 자격이 주어진다. AMC10의 경우는 Algebra2 절반정도 AMC12의 경우에는 Precalculus를 2/3정도 배운 학생이면 충분히 공부해볼만 하다.

매년 2월에만 2회 실시가 된다. 특히 10학년 이하의 학생들은 AMC10에 응시하던가 아니면 한번은 AMC12에 응시하는 것이 좋다. 무조건 AMC12에만 응시하는 것은 좋지 않다. AMC10에 응시할 수 있는 기회는 10학년때 까지 이기 때문이다. 그 이후에는 응시하고 싶어도 무조건 AMC12에만 응시해야 한다. AMC를 통과하면 AIME시험을 봐야하는데 Usamo 또는 Usjmo 진출자는 AMC와 AIME성적 합산으로 선발되므로 AMC10을 응시할 수 있을 때 응시 하는 것이 좋다. 실제로 미국 대학 입시에서는 AMC10과 AMC12를 크게 구분하지 않는다.

Preface

필자는 한국의 수능수학과 경시수학을 강의하던 강사였다. 우연한 기회에 외고생에게 SAT와 AP과목을 가르치면서 미국수학분야에서 일하게 되었다. 수능과 경시를 가르칠 때 이미 AMC문제들과 AIME문제들을 활용을 한 적이 있었다. 실제로 한국의 수능시험을 보면 그 모델이 AMC와 AIME라는 점을 느끼게 된다.

미국내에서는 AMC 이외에도 여러 수학경시가 실시가 된다. 필자는 매년 나오는 그 문제들을 놓치지 않고 모두 풀어보려 노력한다. 여러 문제들을 풀다보면 너무나 좋다고 느껴졌던 문제들은 어김없이 AMC에 반영되어 출제가 된다. 그만큼 AMC의 문제들은 학생들의 수학 실력을 진정으로 올려줄 수 있는 문제들로만 구성이 되어있다.

1990년대부터 최근의 AMC기출문제까지 그리고 1983년부터 지금까지의 AIME를 여러 번 반복해서 풀어보고 그 이외의 다른 경시들까지도 꼼꼼히 풀어보면서 항상 최상의 문제들을 선별하려 노력을 해왔다. 제자들 중 AMC와 AIME에서 좋은 결과가 있었던 학생들은 기계적으로 기출문제만 풀었던 학생들이 아니다. 선별된 250~300문제정도를 반복하여 여러 번 풀어봤던 학생들이 결과가 좋았었다.

이번에 내놓는 새로운 AMC교재는 수년간 수업현장에서 가장 도움이 많이 되었다고 판단되는 문제들만 실었다. AMC기출문제뿐만 아니라 다른 수학경시 문제들도 상당 수 실려 있다. 매번 수업자료를 업그레이드 시키면서 생긴 아이디어와 수업 중에 문득 떠 오른 아이디어 그 어느 하나도 안 놓치고 이 책에 모두 실으려고 노력을 하였다.

그 동안 AMC, AIME강의를 준비하고 교재를 준비하는 과정에서 본인이 할 수 있는 모든 노력은 다했다고 자신있게 말씀 드릴 수 있다.

마지막으로 필자와 같이 TOP SEM학원에서 강의하시는 모든 선생님들과 직원분들께 지면을 빌려 감사한 마음을 전한다. 이 책의 동영상 강의를 허락해주신 마스터프렙 권주근 대표님께도 감사드린다. 소중한 자녀들을 맡겨주신 학부모님들과 본인을 믿고 따라주는 학생들에게도 감사한 마음을 전한다.

이 책이 모든 학생들에게 꼭 필요한 중요한 길잡이가 되기를 간절히 바라는 바이다.

2017. 11. 16
심 현 성

심선생의 한마디!!

1. AMC를 왜 준비하여야 하는가?

필자는 수업현장에서 다음과 같은 말을 많이 듣는다. "제가 아는 원장님이 AIME도 통과 못할 것이면 아예 하지 말라는데요?".....정말 어이가 없는 질문이다. 그런 말씀을 하시는 원장님들은 과연 대학원서를 한번이라도 보기는 한 걸까? 물론 AIME를 통과한다는 것은 상당히 어렵고 많은 시간을 요구한다. 필자는 이렇게 말씀드리고 싶다. AMC10 이든지 AMC12이든지 턱걸이라도 성적을 만들자고 말이다. 단지 성적을 잘 내는 것도 중요하겠지만 AMC를 통해 할 수 있는 것이 너무나 많다. 시도조차 안하면 확률은 0%이고 시도를 하면 확률이 있는 것이다. AMC성적이 높다하여 명문대에 진학한다는 보장은 없다. 하지만, 명문대에 진학하고자 하는 학생이라면 본인이 할 수 있는 모든 것에 도전을 해야 한다. 좋은 대학은 그냥 얻어지는 것이 아니라 노력하고 도전하는 자에게 주어지게 되는 것이다. 뿐만 아니라 AMC10 또는 AMC12를 공부했던 학생들이 교과에 큰 도움이 된다고도 하며 심지어 대학에 진학한 학생들마저도 대학에서 배우는 수학이 AMC 같다고도 한다. 일일이 나열하면 너무 많기에 몇 가지만 말씀드리려고 한다.

1. 미국 보딩스쿨에 다니는 여학생들의 경우 미국 내 여학생순위 300등안에 들면 여름방학 전에 MIT Girl Math대회에 참가하라는 초대장이 온다. 물론 이 대회에서 입상하기란 하늘의 별따기이다. 중요한 것은 이 여학생들의 명단이 몇몇 대학에서 공유가 된다는 점이다. 그렇다면 300명안에 드는 것이 어려운 일인가?...절대 아니다. 입상성적 커트라인보다 조금만 높아도 초대장을 받게 된다. MIT에 진학한 한 여학생의 말에 따르면 MIT에 다니는 한국 학생들이나 동양계 학생들 모두 MIT Girl Math대회에서 봤던 학생들이라고 한다. 뿐만 아니라 근래에 들어서는 MIT Girl Math대회에 참가했던 학생들에게 UCLA에서 단체 메일을 보냈다고 한다. 그 조건은 본교 수학과에 지원하면 4년 장학금을 주겠다는 내용이었다.

2. 미국 내에는 여러 썸머캠프가 있다. 그 중에서도 특히 경쟁력이 강한 몇몇 캠프가 있는데 이 캠프에 들어가기도 대학 들어가는 것 만큼 어렵다. 대신 대학 진학시 확실한 스펙이 되기에 도전해 볼 만하다. 특히, 여러 분야중 수학캠프가 가장 많다. 비즈니스 캠프라면 누구나 도전해 보는 캠프가 유펜에서 진행하는 Jerome Fisher인데 원서를 보면 500자 에세이와 되도록 수학 과학 교사의 추천서를 받으라는 내용과 SAT,ACT성적..그리고 엑스트라 3가지를 써 내라고 한다. SAT가 고득점인 학생들은 아무 생각 없이 무작정 지원을 하는데 대부분이 떨어진다. Jerome Fisher는 SAT성적으로 뽑는 캠프가 아니다. 500자 에세이도 중요하지만 사실상 더 중요한 것은 엑스트라 3개에 수학과학 분야에서 뛰어난 것을 적어내야 한다.
지금까지 이 캠프에 합격했던 학생들의 경우 모두 AMC10 또는 AMC12 입상성적이 있었던 학생들이다.

3. 학교 교사들의 관심을 받을 수 있다.
몇 해 전 AMC12에서 104점으로 입상을 한 학생이 있었는데 그 학교 교장선생님께서 부모님까지 초대하여 상장을 주었다. 우리 학교에 이런 학생이 있었다는 것에 자부심을 느낀다면서 추천서를 써주셨다고 한다.
학교마다 차이는 있겠지만 교장선생님의 추천서를 받는 학생들도 종종 있었다.

4. 다음은 각 대학 원서중의 일부를 발췌한 것이다 대학들은 이런 식으로 AMC성적을
요구한다. 몇몇 주요 대학의 원서를 캡처하였다. 참고하기 바란다.

A. MIT

5. [_____]   ⃝ School ⃝ Regional ⃝ State ⃝ National ⃝ Interna

If you have taken the AMC 10, AMC 12, or AIME exams, list dates and scores. (If you haven't taken these exams or
they are, don't worry about it.)

	Date (MM/YYYY)	Score		Date (MM/YYYY)	Score
AMC 12			AIME		
AMC 10			AIME		

[Save] [Save and Continue]   **Section Four**

B. Caltech

Is English your native language and/or have you had two or
more years of school instruction in English? *

⦿ Yes

⃝ No

Clear

Have you taken math exams, such as the AMC 12 or
AIME? If so, please list your scores and their corresponding
dates.

| Select ▲ |
| Yes |
| No |

Have you taken math exams, such as the AMC 12
AIME? If so, please list your scores and their
corresponding dates.

| Yes | × ▾ |

AMC 12

Score

[_____]

Test Date

[Month ▾] [Day ▾] [Year ▾]

AMC 12

Score

[_____]

Test Date

[Month ▾] [Day ▾] [Year ▾]

AIME

Score

C. Yale

Words entered: 0

Please list any **additional** academic examinations you have taken or will take, **other than those already listed in the Testing section of the Common Application**, such as the SAT, ACT, national/international final exams (e.g., A-Levels, International Baccalaureate, school leaving certificates) or subject area exams (e.g., American Mathematical Competitions-- AMC/AIME, etc.). Include the name of the examination, the month and year taken or planned, and the score received. If your school makes **predictions** for these additional exams (A-Levels, IB, leaving exams, etc.), please note them here.

D. CMU

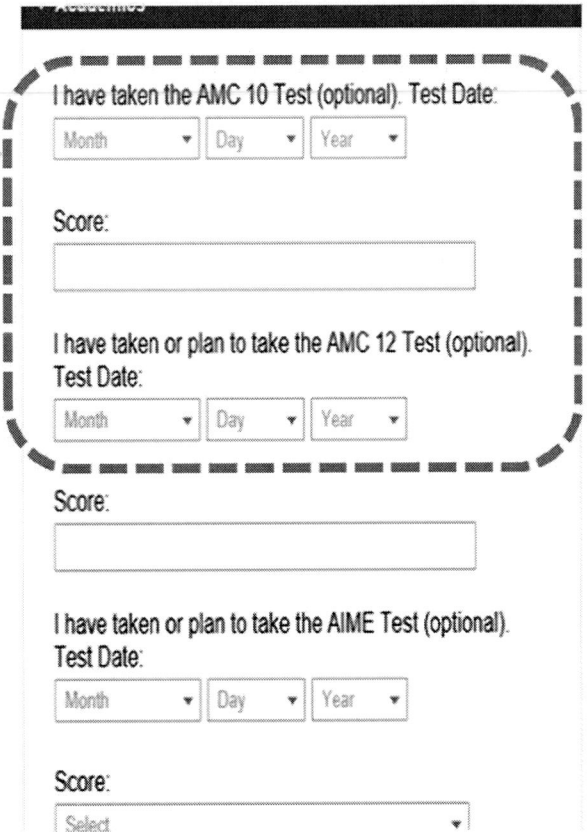

I have taken the AMC 10 Test (optional). Test Date:

Month | Day | Year

Score:

I have taken or plan to take the AMC 12 Test (optional).
Test Date:

Month | Day | Year

Score:

I have taken or plan to take the AIME Test (optional).
Test Date:

Month | Day | Year

Score:

Select

E. Brown

If you intend to apply to the Program in Liberal Medical Education or the Brown RISD Dual Degree Program, please indicate your interest by selecting the program here. *

Select ▼

Some schools offer students the opportunity to take national exams in areas such as math and language. These exams include, but are not limited to, AIME, AMC 10, Le Grand Concours, National Spanish Exam, National Latin Exams. If you have taken any of these exams (or any other subject-based national or international examinations), please inform us of the exams and scores you find most meaningful.

앞에서 살펴 본 것처럼 주요 여러 대학들이 AMC성적을 쓰도록 권장하고 있다.

앞에서 나열한 몇 가지 이유 외에도 많은 이유들이 있다. 하지만 너무나 당연한 것들이라서 여기까지만 하기로 한다. AIME를 통과하지 못할 것이면 아예 시작도 하지 말라는 것은 변명으로 밖에 안 들린다. 우리 학원에 AMC 선생님이 없거나 학부모님과 학생의 입장에서는 공부할 자신이 없던가...

2. 기계식으로 기출문제만 푸는 공부는 실력 향상에 도움이 안 된다!

필자에게 수업을 듣는 학생들 중 혼자서 또는 학원에서 기출문제 10년치 이상을 풀었다는 학생들을 자주 만난다. 참 이상한 것이 수업을 하다보면 분명히 풀었던 문제인데도 아예 답조차 모르고 있는 경우가 많다. 학생이나 학부모님들과 대화를 나누어 보면 1번부터 17번까지는 쉬운데 그 이후부터는 어려워서 잘 못 푼다고 한다.

 그렇다면 기출문제를 두 배로 늘려 더 많이 풀어보면 이 일이 해결될 것인가? 대답은 절대 NO~!이다. 수학은 푸는 개념이 아니다. Writing이다. 단어가 있어야 문장이 만들어 지는 것처럼 Variable을 가지고 Equation을 만드는 것이다. 여기서 우리가 배우는 Variable의 종류는 몇 개 안된다. Real Number, Complex Number, Trigonometry, Vector...등 7가지가 채 안 된다. 우리는 교과에서 Variable 즉, 단어를 배우는 것이고 AMC 는 이 단어들을 활용하여 Equation을 쓰는 시험인 것이다. 고득점자 학생들의 말은 "1번 문제는 적을게 적어보이고 20번 문제이후는 쓸 것이 많아 보인다."라고들 한다. 수입을 하다보면 문제가 조금만 쉬우면 풀이를 쓰지도 않고 눈대중으로 찍는 학생들이 있는데 이럴 경우 필자에게 엄청난 꾸지람을 듣게 된다. 수학을 잘하는 학생은 1번 문제나 25번 문제나 AMC8 문제나 쓰는 양이 일정하다. 이는 어떠한 문제라도 꼼꼼히 쓰는 연습을 했던 학생들만이 가능한 것이다. 또한 같은 문제들을 여러 번 반복해서 써봐야 실력이 는다. 수학적인 머리와 창의력이라는 것은 머릿속에 주입된 상태와 반복훈련에 의해 나오는 것이다. 제자들 중 130점 이상의 고득점자들은 같은 문제 250개 정도를 3~5번 이상 반복하여 공부하였던 학생들이다.

◆ Contents ◆

Chapter 1

➤Algebra

1, 2, 2, 2, 3, 3, a, b, 11

01. In the data above, respectively, the least number is 1 and the greatest number is
    The median of the list is 3 and the mode of the list is 2. Which of the following
    could be the average (arithmetic mean) of the numbers in the list?

    I. 3
    II. 4
    III. 4.5

    (A) I only
    (B) II only
    (C) I and III only
    (D) II and III only
    (E) I, II and III

02. At a certain farm, total 85 chicks were hatched during October. On October 10th,
    the number of the chicks hatched was the greatest. What is the least number of
    chicks that could have been hatched on October 10th?

    (A) 1
    (B) 2
    (C) 3
    (D) 4
    (E) 5

10

03. The original price of a *CD* was *C* dollars. The price was discounted 30 percent during a sale. Emily used a coupon to buy the *CD* for *r* percent off the sale price. Which of the following represents the price, in dollars, that Emily paid for the *CD*?

(A) $(0.3)\left(1 - \dfrac{r}{100}\right)C$

(B) $(0.7)\left((1 - \dfrac{r}{100}\right)C$

(C) $(0.7)\left(\dfrac{1 - r}{100}\right)C$

(D) $C(0.7)\left(\dfrac{r}{100}\right)$

(E) $C\left(\dfrac{0.7r}{100}\right)$

04. Benton and Jane are both salespeople. Benton's monthly compensation consists of $1,000 plus 10 percent of his sales. Jane's monthly compensation consists of $900 plus 15 percent of her sales. If they both had the same amount of sales and the same compensation for a particular month, what was that compensation, in dollars?

(A) 1200
(B) 1400
(C) 1600
(D) 1800
(E) 2000

05. At a certain school, 30 percent of the student population are girls, and the 20 percent of the girls wore glasses. If 72 girls didn't wear glasses, then what is the total number of the student population?

    (A) 100

    (B) 200

    (C) 300

    (D) 400

    (E) 500

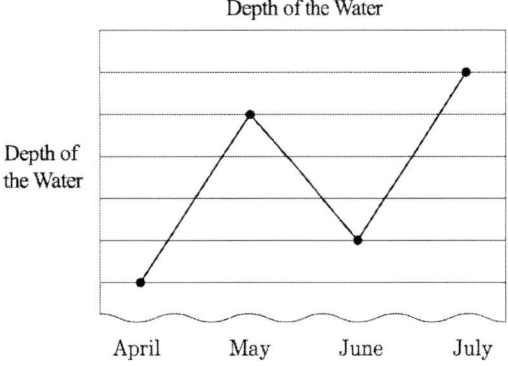

06. Ella tracked the depth of the water in a cylinder from April to July. Each unit on the vertical axis represents 3 centimeters. If the depth of the water decreased 30 percent from May to June, what was the depth of the water on June?

    (A) 9cm

    (B) 12cm

    (C) 15cm

    (D) 21cm

    (E) 22cm

07. Jim earns three thousand dollars per month and he saves 20% of his salary. Last year on January 1st, he saved 10 thousand dollars in his saving account and on 31 of December, he received 860 dollars of interest. The yearly rate of interest is $\cdots$

   (A) 25%
   (B) 5%
   (C) 7.5%
   (D) 10%
   (E) 12.5%

08. Jim is a car salesman who gets a base monthly salary and a commission for each car he sells. Jim's monthly earnings are given by the function $f(x) = c(4 + x)$, where x represents the number of cars he sold for the month. If Jim sells 6 cars in a month, he earns $2,000. How much is Jim's base salary?

   (A) $200
   (B) $600
   (C) $700
   (D) $800
   (E) $900

09. A group of people were standing single file in a line to buy hamburgers. As Rosa stood in the line, she noticed that there were 5 less people behind her than there were in front of her. She also noticed that the total number of people in the line was 3 times the number of people behind her. How many people were in the line?

(A) 16
(B) 18
(C) 20
(D) 22
(E) 24

10. A taxi charges k dollars for the first 3 kilometers and charges for any additional distance at the rate of t dollars per kilometer. If a certain passenger rode more than 3 kilometers and paid $100, which represents the total distance that the taxi traveled?

(A) $\dfrac{100}{k} - 3t$

(B) $\dfrac{100 + k - 3t}{t}$

(C) $\dfrac{100}{t + k} - 3$

(D) $\dfrac{100 - k + 3t}{t}$

(E) $\dfrac{100 + k}{t} - 3t$

11. Each student in a group of 30 students studies World History, Math or both. The total number of students studying World History is three more than the total number of students studying Math. If the number of students that study both subjects is the same as the number of students that study exactly one subject, how many students in the group study only Math?

   (A) 6
   (B) 9
   (C) 15
   (D) 21
   (E) 24

12. Rosa decides to go on a trip with $480 of spending money. She plans to use 25% of her trip expense on the hotel rooms. She will be sharing the cost equally with her 4 other friends. If Rosa and her friends will be using two rooms of the same cost, what is the cost of one hotel room?

   (A) $80
   (B) $120
   (C) $240
   (D) $300
   (E) $360

13. m students agreed to contribute equally to a dinner that costs c dollars. If b of the students fail to contribute, which of the following represents the additional amount, in dollars, that each of the remaining students must contribute to pay for the dinner?

(A) $\dfrac{bc}{m(m-b)}$

(B) $\dfrac{bc}{m-b}$

(C) $\dfrac{b}{m(m-b)}$

(D) $\dfrac{c}{m-b}$

(E) $\dfrac{c}{m}$

14. The state income tax where Kristin lives is levied at the rate of $p\%$ of the first $\$28000$ of annual income plus $(p+2)\%$ of any amount above $\$28000$. Kristin noticed that the state income tax she paid amounted to $(p+0.25)\%$ of her annual income. What was her annual income?

(A) $\$28,000$

(B) $\$32,000$

(C) $\$35,000$

(D) $\$42,000$

(E) $\$56,000$

15. Joe and JoAnn each bought 12 ounces of coffee in a 16 ounce cup. Joe drank 2 ounces of his coffee and then added 2 ounces of cream. JoAnn added 2 ounces of cream, stirred the coffee well, and then drank 2 ounces. What is the resulting ratio of the amount of cream in Joe's coffee to that in JoAnn's coffee?

(A) $\dfrac{6}{7}$

(B) $\dfrac{13}{14}$

(C) 1

(D) $\dfrac{14}{13}$

(E) $\dfrac{7}{6}$

16. Doug can paint a room in 5 hours. Dave can paint the same room in 7 hours. Doug and Dave paint the room together and take a one-hour break for lunch. Let t be the total time, in hours, required for them to complete the job working together, including lunch. Which of the following equations is satisfied by t?

(A) $\left(\dfrac{1}{5}+\dfrac{1}{7}\right)(t+1)=1$

(B) $\left(\dfrac{1}{5}+\dfrac{1}{7}\right)t+1=1$

(C) $\left(\dfrac{1}{5}+\dfrac{1}{7}\right)t=1$

(D) $\left(\dfrac{1}{5}+\dfrac{1}{7}\right)(t-1)=1$

(E) $(5+7)t=1$

17. Bricklayer Brenda would take nine hours to build a chimney alone, and bricklayer Brandon would take 10 hours to build it alone. When they work together, they talk a lot, and their combined output decreases by 10 bricks per hour. Working together, they build the chimney in 5 hours. How many bricks are in the chimney?

(A) 500

(B) 900

(C) 950

(D) 1000

(E) 1900

18. Angelina drove at an average rate of 80 kph and then stopped 20 minutes for gas. After the stop, she drove at an average rate of 100 kph. Altogether she drove 250 km in a total trip time of 3 hours including the stop. Which equation could be used to solve for the time t in hours that she drove before her stop?

(A) $80t + 100(\frac{8}{3} - t) = 250$

(B) $80t = 250$

(C) $100t = 250$

(D) $90t = 250$

(E) $80(\frac{8}{3} - t) + 100t = 250$

19. The players on a basketball team made some three-point shots, some two-point shots, and some one-point free throws. They scored as many points with two-point shots as with three-point shots. Their number of successful free throws was one more than their number of successful two-point shots. The team's total score was 61 points. How many free throws did they make?

(A) 13
(B) 14
(C) 15
(D) 16
(E) 17

20. Tom's age is T years, which is also the sum of the ages of his three children. His age N years ago was twice the sum of their ages then. What is T/N?

(A) 2
(B) 3
(C) 4
(D) 5
(E) 6

1. 미적분학의 발견

미분학은 곡선에의 접선을 긋는 것으로부터, 그리고 적분학은 곡선으로 둘러싸인 부분의 면적을 구하는 것으로부터 시작되었다고 할 수 있고, 이것들은 그리스 시대에도 논해지기는 했었다. 그러나 그리스 사람들이 생각한 접선이란 예컨대 원에 대해서는 원과 한 점을 공유하고 있지만, 그 이외의 점을 공유하지 않는 직선이란 의미이고 이 정의는 말하자면 정적이었다. 이 접선의 개념은 데스카르트와 페르마에 의해서 진일보되기는 했으나 정적인 범위를 벗어나지 못했었다. 이 정적인 생각을 넘어서서 동적으로 생각하여 움직이는 수학이라 할 수 있는 미분적분학을 건설한 것은 영국의 뉴톤(1642-1727)과 독일의 라이프니지(1646-1716)이었다. 미분적분학에 관한 계산법에 관해서는 라이프니지와의 사이에 그 선취권에 관한 논쟁이 있기도 했었다. 그러나 발표는 라이프니지 쪽이 앞섰지만, 실은 이미 그 10여년전에 뉴톤이 발표, 연구하고 있었다는 사실이 후대에 와서 밝혀지기도 했다.

라이프니지는 1673년경에 4분원의 면적을 $\pi/4 = 1 - 1/3 + 1/5 - 1/7 + 1/9 - \cdots$로 구했다.

2. π의 역사

원은 어떤 반지름의 원을 그려도 언제나 같은 모양이다. 따라서 원의 둘레의 길이와 지름의 길이와의 비는 원의 크기에 관계없이 모두 같게 되는데, 이 비의 값이 바로 원주율 π이다.

고대 바빌로니아 사람들은 원주율의 근사값으로 3을 썼다. 가장 오래된 수학책으로 알려진 이집트의 수학자 아메스의 파피루스에는 원주율이 $(16/9)^2 = 3.16049 \cdots$ 로 계산되어 있어 π에 가깝다. 이론적으로 그리스의 수학자 아르키메데스는 원에 내접, 외접하는 정육각형에서 시작하여 정구십육각형까지 를 작은 쪽과 큰 쪽으로 나누어 계산하여 $223/71 (= 3.1408 \cdots) < \pi < 22/7 (= 3.1428 \cdots)$이라는 부등식을 얻었다. 그 후 중국의 수학자 조충지는 π가 3.1415926보다 크고 3.1415927보다 작다는 결론을 이끌어냈다. 그 뒤를 이어 프랑스의 수학자 비에트는 3.1415926535 $\cdots$.

다시 네덜란드의 루돌프는 3.14159265358979323846264338327950288419 $\cdots$라는 것을 알아냈다. 과연 원주율의 정확한 값은 얼마일까?

Chapter 2

➤Equation

Equation

Root/Solution 이란?

$x-1=0$에서 $x=1$이다. 이를 다음의 Graph에서 보면

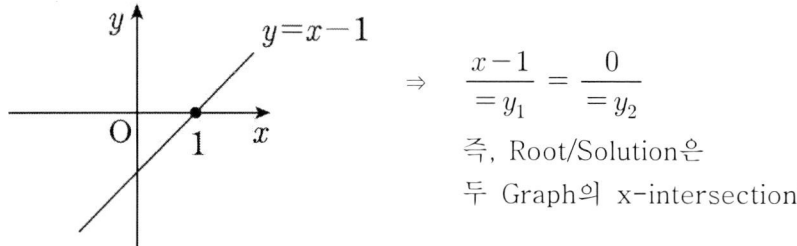

$\Rightarrow \quad \dfrac{x-1}{=y_1} = \dfrac{0}{=y_2}$

즉, Root/Solution은
두 Graph의 x-intersection!

Vieta's Formula

$ax^2+bx+c=0$에서 $x=\dfrac{-b\pm\sqrt{b^2-4ac}}{2a}$ 이므로

두 개의 x값을 더하면 $-\dfrac{b}{a}$이고 곱하면 $\dfrac{c}{a}$가 된다.

그러므로,

1. $ax^2+bx+c=0$의 두 root를 α, β라고 하면

   • $\alpha+\beta=-\dfrac{b}{a}$ • $\alpha\beta=\dfrac{c}{a}$

2. Leading Coefficient가 1이고 두 root를 α, β라고 하면,

   $(x-\alpha)(x-\beta)=0 \Rightarrow x^2-(\alpha+\beta)x+\alpha\beta=0$

다음의 Vieta's Formula에 대해서도 모두 알아 두어야 한다.

1. $ax^3 + bx^2 + cx + d = 0$의 Root를 α, β, γ라고 하면

$$\underbrace{\alpha + \beta + \gamma = -\frac{b}{a}}_{\text{모든 합}} \qquad \underbrace{\alpha\beta + \beta\gamma + \gamma\alpha = \frac{c}{a}}_{\substack{\text{두 개씩} \\ \text{두 개끼리의 곱!}}} \qquad \underbrace{\alpha\beta\gamma = -\frac{d}{a}}_{\text{몽땅 곱!}}$$

2. $ax^4 + bx^3 + cx^2 + dx + e = 0$의 Root를 $x_q\, x_2\, x_3\, x_4$라고 하면,

$$\underbrace{x_1 + x_2 + x_3 + x_4 = -\frac{b}{a}}_{\text{모든 합}} \qquad \underbrace{x_1x_2 + x_1x_3 + x_1x_4 + x_2x_3 + x_3x_4 = \frac{c}{a}}_{\text{두 개씩 곱!}}$$

$$\underbrace{x_1x_2x_3 + x_1x_2x_4 + x_1x_3x_4 + x_2x_3x_4 = -\frac{d}{a}}_{\text{세 개씩 곱!}}$$

$$\underbrace{x_1x_2x_3x_4 = \frac{e}{a}}_{\text{몽땅 곱!}}$$

앞에서 보는 바와 같이 Vieta's Formula는 어느 정도 규칙이 있다.

반드시 알아두자!

---

① +, -, +, - 순으로 나간다.
② 처음에는 모든 Root를 Sum하고 그 다음에는
   두 개씩, 세 개씩, 네 개씩... 끼리끼리 곱해서 더하고
   마지막에는 몽땅 곱한다.

다음을 반드시 암기하자!

- $ma+mb=m(a+b)$

- $a^2-b^2=(a-b)(a+b)$

- $a^2+b^2=(a+b)^2-2ab$
  $\quad\quad\quad=(a-b)^2+2ab$

- $a^3+b^3=(a+b)^3-3ab(a+b)$
  $\quad\quad\quad=(a+b)(a^2-ab+b^2)$

- $a^3-b^3=(a-b)^3+3ab(a-b)$
  $\quad\quad\quad=(a-b)(a^2+ab+b^2)$

- $(a+b+c)^2=a^2+b^2+c^2+2(ab+bc+ca)$

- $a^3+b^3+c^3-3abc$
  $\quad\quad\quad=(a+b+c)(a^2+b^2+c^2-ab-bc-ca)$

01. Let f be a function for which $f\left(\dfrac{x}{3}\right) = x^2 + x + 1$. Find the sum of all values of z for which $f(3z) = 7$.

(A) $-\dfrac{1}{3}$

(B) $-\dfrac{1}{9}$

(C) 0

(D) $\dfrac{5}{9}$

(E) $\dfrac{5}{3}$

02. What is the sum of all of the roots of $(2x+3)(x-4)+(2x+3)(x-6)=0$?

(A) $7/2$

(B) 4

(C) 5

(D) 7

(E) 13

03. Both roots of the quadratic equation $x^2 - 63x + k = 0$ are prime numbers. The number of possible values of k is

    (A) 0

    (B) 1

    (C) 2

    (D) 4

    (E) more than 4

04. Let d and e denote the solutions of $2x^2 + 3x - 5 = 0$. What is the value of $(d-1)(e-1)$?

    (A) $-\dfrac{5}{2}$

    (B) 0

    (C) 3

    (D) 5

    (E) 6

05. What is the sum of the reciprocals of the roots of the equation $\frac{2003}{2004}x + 1 + \frac{1}{x} = 0$?

(A) $-\frac{2004}{2003}$

(B) -1

(C) $\frac{2003}{2004}$

(D) 1

(E) $\frac{2004}{2003}$

06. Let $a+1 = b+2 = c+3 = d+4 = a+b+c+d+5$. What is $a+b+c+d$?

(A) -5

(B) $-10/3$

(C) $-7/3$

(D) $5/3$

(E) 5

07. Let a and b be the roots of the equation $x^2 - mx + 2 = 0$. Suppose that $a + \dfrac{1}{b}$ and $b + \dfrac{1}{a}$ are the roots of the equation $x^2 - px + q = 0$. What is q?

(A) $\dfrac{5}{2}$

(B) $\dfrac{7}{2}$

(C) 4

(D) $\dfrac{9}{2}$

(E) 8

08. The quadratic equation $x^2 + mx + n$ has roots twice those of $x^2 + px + m$, and none of m, n, and p is zero. What is the value of n/p?

(A) 1

(B) 2

(C) 4

(D) 8

(E) 16

09. The graph of the function f is shown below. How many solutions does the equation $f(f(x)) = 6$ have?

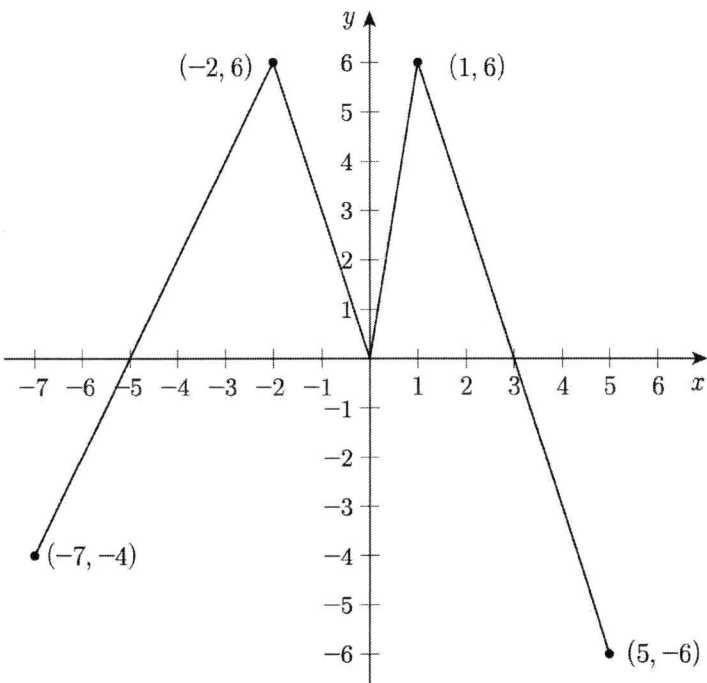

(A) 2

(B) 4

(C) 5

(D) 6

(E) 7

10. The graph of the polynomial $P(x) = x^5 + ax^4 + bx^3 + cx^2 + dx + e$ has five distinct x−intercepts, one of which is at $(0, 0)$. Which of the following coefficients cannot be zero?

    (A) a

    (B) b

    (C) c

    (D) d

    (E) e

11. Let f be a function with the following properties :

    (i) $f(1) = 1$, and

    (ii) $f(2n) = n \times f(n)$, for any positive integer n.

    What is the value of $f(2^{100})$?

    (A) 1

    (B) 2^{99}

    (C) 2^{100}

    (D) 2^{4950}

    (E) 2^{9999}

12. Let $P(x) = (x-1)(x-2)(x-3)$. For how many polynomials $Q(x)$ does there exist a polynomial $R(x)$ of degree 3 such that $P(Q(x)) = P(x) \times R(x)$?

(A) 19

(B) 22

(C) 24

(D) 27

(E) 32

13. The nonzero coefficients of a polynomial P with real coefficients are all replaced by their mean to form a polynomial Q. Which of the following could be a graph of $y = P(x)$ and $y = Q(x)$ over the interval $-4 \le x \le 4$?

(A)

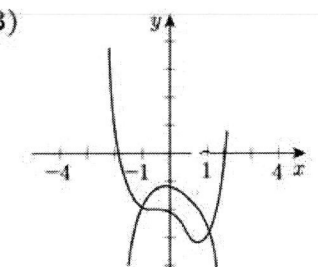

(B)

(C)

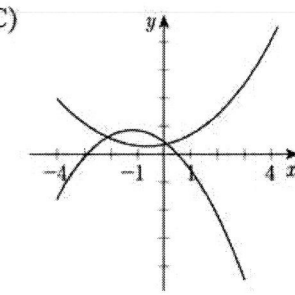

(D)

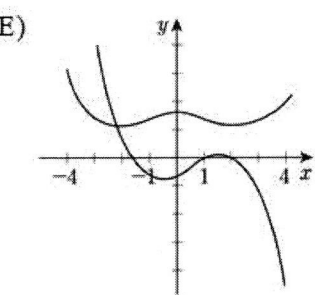

(E)

14. If a, b, c, d, and e are constants such that all real numbers x satisfies

$$\frac{5x^4 - 8x^3 + 2x^2 + 4x + 7}{(x+2)^4} = a + \frac{b}{x+2} + \frac{c}{(x+2)^2} + \frac{d}{(x+2)^3} + \frac{e}{(x+2)^4},$$

then what is the value of $a+b+c+d+e$?

(A) 12

(B) 14

(C) 16

(D) 18

(E) 20

15. Let a, b, c, x, y, and z be real numbers that satisfy the three equations

$$13x + by + cz = 0$$
$$ax + 23y + cz = 0$$
$$ax + by + 42z = 0$$

Suppose that $a \neq 13$ and $x \neq 0$. What is the value of $\dfrac{13}{a-13} + \dfrac{23}{b-23} + \dfrac{42}{c-42}$?

(A) 1

(B) 0

(C) -1

(D) -2

(E) -4

16. A triangle has sides of length $\sqrt{13}$, $\sqrt{17}$, and $2\sqrt{5}$. What is the area of the triangle?

(A) $\sqrt{13}$

(B) $3\sqrt{3}$

(C) $\sqrt{37}$

(D) $\sqrt{47}$

(E) 7

17. Let P be a cubic polynomial with $P(0) = k$, $P(1) = 2k$, and $P(-1) = 3k$. What is $P(2) + P(-2)$?

(A) 0

(B) k

(C) $6k$

(D) $7k$

(E) $14k$

18. Let a, b, c, d be real numbers such that $ad + bc = 44$ and $a^2 + b^2 = \dfrac{2017}{c^2 + d^2}$. What is the possible value of $ac - bd$?

 (A) -3

 (B) 3

 (C) 9

 (D) 27

 (E) 81

19. Let a be a positive real number such that $a^2 + \dfrac{16}{a^2} = 2017$. What is the value of

 $\sqrt{a} + \dfrac{2}{\sqrt{a}}$?

 (A) 3

 (B) 4

 (C) 5

 (D) 6

 (E) 7

20. Let a be a real number such that $4^{2a+1} + (\dfrac{1}{4})^{2a-1} = 2017$. What is the value of

 $2^{a+1} + (\dfrac{1}{2})^{a-1}$?

 (A) $\sqrt{2}$

 (B) $\sqrt{3}$

 (C) $4\sqrt{2}$

 (D) $7\sqrt{2}$

 (E) 49

21. Solve in real numbers the system of equations

$$\begin{cases} x-y=87 \\ \sqrt{2017-x}+\sqrt{2018-y}=22 \end{cases}$$. Choose the right answer.

(A) $x=1936,\ y=1849$

(B) $x=1937,\ y=1850$

(C) $x=1938,\ y=1851$

(D) $x=1939,\ y=1852$

(E) $x=1940,\ y=1853$

22. Let a be a real number greater than 1 such that $22(a+\dfrac{1}{a})=\sqrt{2017}$. What is the value of $a-\dfrac{1}{a}$?

(A) $\dfrac{1}{22}$

(B) $\dfrac{9}{22}$

(C) 22

(D) 44

(E) 484

23. Solve the equation $2^{6x+1}-4^{3x+3}+8^{2x+4}=2017$. What is the x?

(A) $-\dfrac{1}{4}$

(B) $-\dfrac{1}{6}$

(C) $-\dfrac{1}{8}$

(D) $-\dfrac{1}{10}$

(E) 0

24. Solve in real numbers the equation $\sqrt[3]{1350x^3+2017+\dfrac{8}{x^3}}=15x^2$. What is x?

(A) -6

(B) -3

(C) -1

(D) 0

(E) 1

36

Chapter 3

➤Integer 1

Integer

"Integer = Counting Number"
즉, Integer는 직접 찾을 수 있는 Number이다.

다음의 두 경우를 보자.

❶ $\begin{cases} x+y =3 \\ x-y =1 \end{cases}$ 　　　　　❷ $xy=4$

❶의 경우에는 두 식을 연립하여 x, y 값을 찾을 수 있다. 하지만 ❷의 경우에는 찾을 수 없다. 이유는 Variable의 개수가 Equation의 개수보다 많기 때문이다. 위의 ❷번 문제를 다음과 같이 바꾸어 보자.

❷ $xy=4$ 　　　　$(x, y$ is a positive integer$)$

이 경우에는 $(x,y)=(1,4),(2,2),(4,1)$ 이 된다.

Positive Integer는 직접 찾을 수 있는 Number 이기 때문에 Variable 개수가 Equation의 개수보다 많더라도 직접 구할 수 있다. 이와 같은 Equation을 Indeterminate Equation(부정방정식)이라고 한다.

즉, 다시 생각해보면, 문제에 Equation 이라는 조건이 있으면 Variable 개수에 상관없이 Equation 한 개만 있으면 되는 것이다.

반드시 알아두자!

Integer 문제는 Equation 한 개만 있으면 해결 된다.
Variable 개수는 신경 쓰지 않아도 된다!

Variable 개수가 많고 Equation이 적으면 어렵게 느껴지게 된다. 문제 중에 "Integer"라는 조건이 있으면 Equation이 반드시 한 개 필요하다.

Equation 만들기!

① Variable 개수를 늘려서라도 Equation을 만들자!
   (※이 책에서는 편의상 "Variable(변수) 확장"이라는 말을 쓰기로 한다.)

② Integer를 x, y와 같이 Variable(변수)로 놓는다.
   (⇒ Variable 확장!) ⇒ Variable 모두 직접 찾기 가능!

③ Integer 끼리는 $+, -, \times$를 하여도 Integer가 된다. 이 성질을 이용하여 Equation을 만들 수 있다.

Integer에 대해서...

1.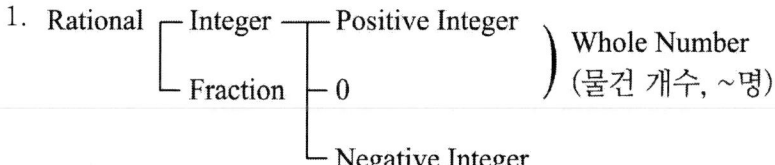

즉, 사람명수, 물건의 개수는 모두 Whole Number이고 모두 직접 찾을 수 있는 Number이다.

2. Digit은 0~9까지의 Integer이다.

3. Prime Number는 factor가 1과 자기 자신인 수이다.

※ Prime Number 판별법

예를 들어, 61은 Prime Number이고 63은 Prime Number가 아니다.

다음과 같이 해보자.

❶ $61 \Rightarrow \sqrt{61} \approx 7.\times\times\times \curvearrowright \sqrt{61}$ 보다 작은 Prime Number로 61을 나누어 보면 2, 3, 5, 7 모두 안 나누어진다. 이때, 61이 Prime Number이다.

❷ $63 \Rightarrow \sqrt{63} \approx 7.\times\times\times \curvearrowright \sqrt{63}$ 보다 작은 Prime Number로 63을 나누어 보면 3으로 나누어진다. 이때, 63은 Prime Number가 아니다.

Factor(약수) Multiple(배수) 인수분해(Factorization)

위의 세 가지 모두 Integer를 빨리 찾기 위한 방법들이다. 이 중에 Multiple(배수) 성질에 대해서 알아보면…

❶ 3의 배수 : 각 digit의 Sum이 3의 배수가 될 때.
❷ 4의 배수 : 마지막 끝 두 자리가 4의 배수가 될 때.
❸ 11의 배수 : 각 자리의 digit을 더하고 빼기를 한 결과가 0 또는 11의 배수가 될 때.

(Example) 10483의 경우
$$\Rightarrow 1-0+4-8+3=0$$
그러므로, 10483은 11의 배수(Multiple)이다.

지금까지의 내용을 정리해보면…

Integer 문제는...

> ① Variable 확장을 해서라도 Equation 한 개를 만든다!
>
> ② Equation을 빨리 해결하기 위해 Factor(약수), Multiple(배수), Factorization (인수분해) 등을 이용한다.

Arithmetic sequence

일정한 차이(Common Difference)가 나는 수들을 배열한 것을 말하며 Integer 문제를 풀 때 필요할 때가 종종 있다.

Arithmetic Sequence

$$a_n = a + (n-1)d$$
$$S_n = \frac{n(a + a_n)}{2}$$

※ a_n : General Term
  a : First Term
  d : Common Difference

- Consecutive Integers : Common Difference 가 1
- Even / odd Integers : Common Difference 가 2
- Multiple of 3 : Common Difference 가 3

01. If $(a-b)^a = 1$ and $b^a = 1$, where a and b are positive integers, what is the value of a?

    (A) 1
    (B) 2
    (C) 3
    (D) 4
    (E) 5

02. If a, b, and c are consecutive integers such that $0 < a < b < c$ and the units (ones) digit of the product ac is 9, which of the following could be the value of b?

    (A) 8
    (B) 9
    (C) 10
    (D) 11
    (E) 12

03. Mr. Jenkin's 2010 algebra class had 5 more students than his 2009 algebra class. The number of students in his 2011 algebra class was exactly 20 percent more than the number of students in his 2010 class. Which of the following could have been the number of students in Mr. Jenkin's 2009 algebra class?

(A) 10
(B) 11
(C) 12
(D) 13
(E) 14

04. A four-digit integer, $ABCD$ in which $A, B, C,$ and D each represent a different digit, is formed according to the following rules

I. $A = B - 2C - D$

II. $B = C + 5$

III. $D = B - 7$

Which of the following could be $ABCD$?

(A) 3720
(B) 1831
(C) 3270
(D) 1813
(E) 1318

05. Three different one-digit positive integers are placed in the bottom row of cells. Numbers in adjacent cells are added and the sum is placed in the cell above them. In the second row, continue the same process to obtain a number in the top cell. What is the difference between the largest and smallest numbers possible in the top cell?

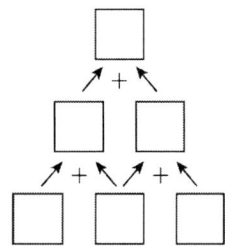

(A) 16

(B) 24

(C) 25

(D) 26

(E) 35

06. In this addition problem, each letter stands for a different digit.

$$\begin{array}{r} T\ W\ O \\ +\ \ T\ W\ O \\ \hline F\ O\ U\ R \end{array}$$

If $T = 7$ and the letter O represents an even number, what is the only possible value for W?

(A) 0

(B) 1

(C) 2

(D) 3

(E) 4

07. The product of three consecutive positive integers is 8 times their sum. What is the sum of their square?

  (A) 50

  (B) 77

  (C) 110

  (D) 149

  (E) 194

08. For how many integers n is $\dfrac{n}{20-n}$ the square of an integer?

  (A) 1

  (B) 2

  (C) 3

  (D) 4

  (E) 10

09. A majority of the 30 girls bought apples. Each of these girls bought the same number of apples, and this number was greater than 1. The cost of apple in cents was greater than the number of apples each girls bought, and the total cost of all the apples was \$17.71. What was the cost of a apple in cents?

(A) 7

(B) 11

(C) 17

(D) 23

(E) 77

10. A charity sells 140 benefit tickets for a total of \$2001. Some tickets sell for full price (a whole dollar amount), and the rest sells for half price. How much money is raised by the full-price tickets?

(A) \$782

(B) \$986

(C) \$1158

(D) \$1219

(E) \$1449

11. How many two-digit positive integers N have the property that the sum of N and the number obtained by reversing the order of the digits of N is a perfect square?

    (A) 4
    (B) 5
    (C) 6
    (D) 7
    (E) 8

12. Let $P(n)$ and $S(n)$ denote the product and the sum, respectively, of the digits of the integer n. For example, $P(23)=6$ and $S(23)=5$. Suppose N is a two-digit number such that $N=P(N)+S(N)$. What is the units digit of N?

    (A) 2
    (B) 3
    (C) 6
    (D) 8
    (E) 9

13. Erika makes N cheeseburgers. For each cheeseburger she uses C globs of cheese at 6 cents per glob and B globs of butter at 7 cents per glob. The cost of the cheese and butter to make all cheeseburgers is \$2.47. If N, C, and B are all positive integers with $N > 1$, which of the following could be the cost of the cheese Erika uses to make the cheeseburgers?

(A) \$1.02
(B) \$1.56
(C) \$2.04
(D) \$2.74
(E) \$3.06

14. In the equation below, A and B are consecutive positive integers, and A, B, and $A + B$ represent number bases:
$$132_A + 43_B = 69_{A+B}$$
What is $A + B$?

(A) 9
(B) 11
(C) 13
(D) 15
(E) 17

48

15. For how many positive integers m does there exist at least one positive integer n such that $m \cdot n \le m+n$?

    (A) 4

    (B) 6

    (C) 9

    (D) 12

    (E) infinitely many

16. Let x and y be two-digit integers such that y is obtained by reversing the digits of x. The integers x and y satisfy $x^2 - y^2 = m^2$ for some positive integer m. What is $x+y+m$?

    (A) 88

    (B) 112

    (C) 116

    (D) 144

    (E) 154

17. A rectangular floor measures a by b feet, where a and b are positive integers with $b > a$. An artist paints a rectangle on the floor with the sides of the rectangle parallel to the sides of the floor. The unpainted part of the floor forms a border of width 1 foot around the painted rectangle and occupies half of the area of the entire floor. How many possibilities are there for the ordered pair (a, b)?

(A) 1
(B) 2
(C) 3
(D) 4
(E) 5

18. Let n be a 5-digit number, and let q and r be the quotient and the remainder, respectively, when n is divided by 100. For how many values of n is $q + r$ divisible by 11?

(A) 8180
(B) 8181
(C) 8182
(D) 9000
(E) 9090

19. In 1980 the rabbit population of a forest was perfect square. Ten years   later, after an increase of 150 rabbits, the population was 9 more than a perfect square. In 2000, with an increase of another 150 rabbits , the population is once again a perfect square. Which of the following is the closest to the percent growth of the forest's population during this twenty-year period?

   (A) 42

   (B) 47

   (C) 52

   (D) 57

   (E) 62

20. Let $f(x) = ax^2 + bx + c$, where a, b, and c are integers. Suppose that $f(1) = 0$, $50 < f(7) < 60$, $70 < f(8) < 80$, and $5000k < f(100) < 5000(k+1)$ for some integer k What is k?

   (A) 1

   (B) 2

   (C) 3

   (D) 4

   (E) 5

21. Suppose a and b are single-digit positive integers chosen independently and at random. What is the probability that the point (a, b) lies above the parabola $y = ax^2 - bx$?

(A) $\dfrac{11}{81}$

(B) $\dfrac{13}{81}$

(C) $\dfrac{5}{27}$

(D) $\dfrac{17}{81}$

(E) $\dfrac{19}{81}$

22. At a competition with N players, the number of players given elite status is equal to $2^{1 + \lfloor \log_2(N-1) \rfloor} - N$. Suppose that 19 players are given elite status. What is the sum of the two smallest possible value of N? (Note: $\lfloor x \rfloor$ is the greatest integer less than or equal to x.)

(A) 38

(B) 90

(C) 154

(D) 406

(E) 1024

23. Four Positive integers a, b, c, and d have a product of $8!$ and satisfy:

$$ab + a + b = 524$$
$$bc + b + c = 146$$
$$cd + c + d = 104$$

What is $a - d$?

(A) 4

(B) 6

(C) 8

(D) 10

(E) 12

24. Let a, b, and c be positive integers with $a \geq b \geq c$ such that

$a^2 - b^2 - c^2 + ab = 2011$ and $a^2 + 3b^2 + 3c^2 - 3ab - 2ac - 2bc = -1997$. What is a?

(A) 249   (B) 250   (C) 251   (D) 252   (E) 253

25. Let a, b, and c be digits with $a \neq 0$. The three-digit integer abc lies one third of the way from the square of a positive integer to the square of the next larger integer. The integer acb lies two thirds of the way between the same two squares. What is $a+b+c$?

    (A) 10

    (B) 13

    (C) 16

    (D) 18

    (E) 21

26. How many non-congruent right triangles with positive integer leg lengths have areas that are numerically equal to 3 times their perimeters?

    (A) 6

    (B) 7

    (C) 8

    (D) 10

    (E) 12

27. How many pairs of positive integers (a, b) are there such that $\gcd(a, b) = 1$ and $\dfrac{a}{b} + \dfrac{14b}{9a}$ is an integer?

  (A) 4

  (B) 6

  (C) 9

  (D) 12

  (E) infinitely many

28. For each positive integer n, let $S(n)$ denote the sum of the digits of n. For how many values of n is $n + S(n) + S(S(n)) = 2007$?

  (A) 1

  (B) 2

  (C) 3

  (D) 4

  (E) 5

29. In how many ways can 345 be written as the sum of an increasing sequence of two or more consecutive positive integers?

(A) 1
(B) 3
(C) 5
(D) 6
(E) 7

30. All the numbers 2, 3, 4, 5, 6, 7 are assigned to the six faces of a cube, one number to each face. For each of the eight vertices of the cube, a product of three numbers is computed, where the three numbers are the numbers assigned to the three faces that include that vertex. What is the greatest possible value of the sum of these eight products?

(A) 312
(B) 343
(C) 625
(D) 729
(E) 1680

31. The zeros of the function $f(x) = x^2 - ax + 2a$ are integers. What is the sum of the possible values of a?

(A) 7

(B) 8

(C) 16

(D) 17

(E) 18

32. Danica drove her new car on a trip for a whold number of hours, averaging 55 miles per hour. At the beginning of the trip, abc miles was displayed on the odometer, where abc is a 3-digit number with $a \geq 1$ and $a + b + c \leq 7$. At the end of the trip, the odometer showed cba miles. What is $a^2 + b^2 + c^2$?

(A) 26

(B) 27

(C) 36

(D) 37

(E) 41

33. How many distinct four-digit numbers are divisible by 3 and have 23 as their last two digits?

    (A) 27

    (B) 30

    (C) 33

    (D) 81

    (E) 90

34. How many four-digit numbers N have the property that the three-digit number obtained by removing the leftmost digit is one ninth of N?

    (A) 4

    (B) 5

    (C) 6

    (D) 7

    (E) 8

35. The arithmetic mean of two distinct positive integers x and y is a two-digit integer. The geometric mean of x and y is obtained by reversing the digits of the arithmetic mean. What is $|x-y|$?

    (A) 24

    (B) 48

    (C) 54

    (D) 66

    (E) 70

36. How many positive integers less than 1000 are 6 times the sum of their digits?

    (A) 0

    (B) 1

    (C) 2

    (D) 4

    (E) 12

37. The first 2007 positive integers are each written in base 3. How many of these base-3 representations are palindromes? (A palindrome is a number that reads the same forward and backward.)

   (A) 100
   (B) 101
   (C) 102
   (D) 103
   (E) 104

38. A palindrome between 1000 and 10,000 is chosen at random. What is the probability that it is divisible by 7?

   (A) $\frac{1}{10}$

   (B) $\frac{1}{9}$

   (C) $\frac{1}{7}$

   (D) $\frac{1}{6}$

   (E) $\frac{1}{5}$

39. How many positive two-digits integers are factors of $2^{24} - 1$?

    (A) 4
    (B) 8
    (C) 10
    (D) 12
    (E) 14

40. For how many n in $\{1, 2, 3, \cdots, 100\}$ is the tens digit of n^2 odd?

    (A) 10
    (B) 20
    (C) 30
    (D) 40
    (E) 50

41. Let x_1, $x2$, . . . , x_n be a sequence of integers such that (i) $-1 \leq x_i \leq 2$ for $i = 1,2,...n$; (ii) $x_1 + \cdots + x_n = 19$; and (iii) $x_1^2 + x_2^2 + \cdots + x_n^2 = 99$. Let m and M be the minimal and maximal possible values of $x_1^3 + \cdots + x_n^3$, respectively. Then, $\dfrac{M}{m} =$

(A) 3
(B) 4
(C) 5
(D) 6
(E) 7

Chapter 4

➤Integer 2

Modulo

Integer는 Counting Number이고
그렇기 때문에 우리는 직접 찾기를 통해 문제를 해결하게 된다.

앞단원에서는 Integer를 직접 찾되 빨리 찾기 위한 수단으로 주고 Multiple과 Factor의 성질을 이용하였다면, 이번 단원에서는 "Modulo(모듈로)"를 이용하는 방법에 대해 소개하고자 한다.

우리는 Integer를 구할 때 가끔 Remainder만 필요한 경우가 있다.
즉, 큰 수를 작게 만들어서 좀 더 편리하고 빠르게 Integer를 구하고자 할 때, 또는 같은 Category에 있는 Integer를 찾고자 할 때 "Modulo"를 이용하게 된다.

본론으로 들어가 보자.

11을 4로 나눈다면 다음과 같이 쓸 것이다.
예를 들어,

① $11 = 4 \cdot 2 + 3$ ② $\dfrac{11}{4} = 2 + \dfrac{3}{4}$

여기에서 Divisor가 2가 되고 Remainder가 3이 된다.
이러한 표현은 다음과 같이 표현한다.

$$11 \bmod 4 = 3$$

예를 들어 11을 4로 나눈 나머지가 3이고 15를 4로 나눈 나머지도 3이 되는데, 이런 경우에는 다음과 같이 표현한다.

$$11 \equiv 15 \pmod 4$$

⇒"11과 15는 모듈 4에 대해 합동 관계"

다음의 간단한 예제들을 보자.

① −6을 7로 나누면?
⇒ $-6 \bmod 7 = 1$

② −9를 4로 나누면?
⇒ $-9 \bmod 4 = 3$
⇒ 이유는 $-9 = 4(-3) + 3$ 이기 때문이다.

다음의 성질들을 간단한 예를 통해 익혀두자.

1) $18 \equiv 13 \pmod 5$, $13 \equiv 8 \pmod 5$
$\Rightarrow$ $18 \equiv 8 \pmod 5$

2) $16 \equiv 11 \pmod 5$, $6 \equiv 1 \pmod 5$
$\Rightarrow$ ① $16 + 6 \equiv 11 + 1 \pmod 5$
$\Rightarrow$ ② $16 \times 6 \equiv 11 \times 1 \pmod 5$
$\Rightarrow$ ③ $16^2 \equiv 11^2 \pmod 5$

   $\quad 16^3 \equiv 11^3 \pmod 5$

   $\quad\quad \vdots$

   $\quad 16^n \equiv 11^n \pmod 5$

3) $2^5 \equiv 2 \pmod 5$
$\Rightarrow$ $2 \cdot 2^5 \equiv 2 \cdot 2 \pmod 5$
$\Rightarrow$ $3 \cdot 2 \cdot 2^5 \equiv 3 \cdot 2 \cdot 2 \pmod 5$

4) $11 \equiv 3 \pmod 4$
$\Rightarrow$ $11 + 2 \equiv 3 + 2 \pmod 4$
$\Rightarrow$ $11 - 1 \equiv 3 - 1 \pmod 4$

5) 100을 12로 나눈다고 해보자.
$100 = 12Q + 4$
$\Rightarrow$ $100 = 2 \cdot 6Q + 4$
$\Rightarrow$ $100 \bmod 2 = 0$ ($100 \equiv 0 \pmod 2$)
$\Rightarrow$ $100 \bmod 6 = 4$ ($100 \equiv 4 \pmod 6$)

즉, 100을 2로 나누면 나머지가 0이고 6으로 나누면 나머지가 4이다.

다음의 몇 가지 규칙 정도는 알아두는 것이 좋다.

1. Perfect Square의 Unit digit은 0, 1, 4, 5, 6, 9이다.

2. n을 Integer라고 할 때, $n^2 \bmod 4 = 0, 1$

3. n을 Integer라고 할 때, $n^2 \bmod 8 = 0, 1, 4$

4. n이 Even Integer이면 $n^2 \equiv 0 \pmod 4$

5. n이 Odd Integer이면 $n^2 \equiv 1 \pmod 4$

6. n이 Prime number라고 하면 2, 3을 제외하고 $6k \pm 1$로 나타낼 수 있다.

7. n이 Prime number이면 $n^2 \equiv 1, 3, 4 \pmod 6$이고 $n^2 \equiv 0 \text{ or } 1 \pmod 4$

학생들의 반응이 문자로 규칙을 알려주는 것보다 숫자로 예를 들어 주는 것이 쉽게 이해가 된다고 하여 숫자로 예를 들어가며 설명하였다.

01. What is the remainder of dividing $2^{20} - 1$ by 41?

    (A) 0

    (B) 1

    (C) 2

    (D) 3

    (E) 4

02. What is the remainder of dividing $1! + 2! + 3! + 4! + \cdots + 99! + 100!$ by 12?

    (A) 7

    (B) 8

    (C) 9

    (D) 10

    (E) 11

03. What is the remainder of dividing 2^{20} by 7?

    (A) 1

    (B) 2

    (C) 3

    (D) 4

    (E) 5

04. What is the remainder of dividing 2^{100} by 13?

    (A) 1
    (B) 2
    (C) 3
    (D) 4
    (E) 5

05. 3^{1234} can be written as $\overline{abcdef.....qr}$. What is the value of $q+r$?

    (A) 11
    (B) 13
    (C) 15
    (D) 17
    (E) 18

06. What is the remainder of dividing 2000^{2000} by 1999?

    (A) 1

    (B) 2

    (C) 3

    (D) 4

    (E) 5

07. Sally's birthday is Sunday, June 10th. What day would it be, 2017^{2017} days after Sally's birth?

    (A) Sunday

    (B) Monday

    (C) Tuesday

    (D) Wednesday

    (E) Thursday

08. Find all primes p and q for which $p^2 + q^2 + 2017$ is a perfect square.

09. If p, q, r are primes such that $p^2 + q^2 + r^2 - 222pqr = 2017$ and $p \geq \max(q, r)$,

evaluate $\dfrac{(p+1)}{(q+1)(r+1)}$.

10. Find all primes p and q such that $p^3 + 27pq^2 - q^3 = 2017$.

11. Let $N = 123456789101112...4344$ be the 79-digit number that is formed by writing the integers from 1 to 44 in order, one after the other. What is the remainder when N is divided by 45?

   (A) 1
   (B) 4
   (C) 9
   (D) 18
   (E) 44

12. Let $S(n)$ equal the sum of the digits of positive integer n. For example, $S(1507) = 13$. For a particular positive integer n, $S(n) = 1274$. Which of the following could be the value of $S(n+1)$?

   (A) 1
   (B) 3
   (C) 12
   (D) 1239
   (E) 1265

13. Last year, Isabella took 7 math tests and received 7 different scores, each an integer between 91 and 100, inclusive. After each test she noticed that the average of her test scores was an integer. Her score on the seventh test was 95. What was her score on the sixth test?

(A) 92
(B) 94
(C) 96
(D) 98
(E) 100

Chapter 5

➤Inequality

Inequality

1. Arithmetic Mean(AM) – Geometric Mean(GM)

- $a+b \geq 2\sqrt{ab}$
- $a+b+c \geq 3\sqrt[3]{abc}$
- $a+b+c+ \ldots +n \geq n\sqrt[n]{abc \ldots n}$

  ($a, b, c \ldots n$은 모두 Positive real number)

(Proof)

$a= \sqrt{a}^2, \ b= \sqrt{b}^2, \ \ \sqrt{ab}= \sqrt{a} \cdot \sqrt{b}$ 이므로

$a+b \geq 2\sqrt{ab} \Rightarrow \sqrt{a}^2 -2\sqrt{a}\sqrt{b}+ \sqrt{b}^2 = (\sqrt{a} - \sqrt{b})^2$

$(\sqrt{a} - \sqrt{b})^2$에서 $a>0, b>0$이고 $a=b$ 라면

$\sqrt{a}^2 -2\sqrt{a}\sqrt{b}+ \sqrt{b}^2 = (\sqrt{a} - \sqrt{b})^2 \geq 0$

2. Schwarz's Inequality

- $(a^2+b^2)(x^2+y^2) \geq (ax+by)^2$
- $(a^2+b^2+c^2)(x^2+y^2+z^2) \geq (ax+by+cz)^2$

  (x, y, z, a, b, c 는 모두 Real number)

(Proof)

$(a^2+b^2)(x^2+y^2) \geq (ax+by)^2$을 전개(Expansion)하면

$a^2x^2+a^2y^2+b^2x^2+b^2y^2 \geq a^2x^2+2abxy+b^2y^2$

$\Rightarrow a^2y^2-2abxy+b^2x^2 = (ay-bx)^2 \geq 0$

74

01. Let a, b and c be real numbers such that $a+b+c=2$, and $a^2+b^2+c^2=12$. What is the difference between the maximum and minimum possible values of c?

(A) 2

(B) $\dfrac{10}{3}$

(C) 4

(D) $\dfrac{16}{3}$

(E) $\dfrac{20}{3}$

02. When four real numbers a, b, c, d satisfy two equations

$$a+b+c+d=6, \quad a^2+b^2+c^2+d^2=12,$$

what is the sum of maximum value and minimum value of $ab+bc+ca$?

(A) 3

(B) 9

(C) 12

(D) 15

(E) 18

03. Suppose $x^3 - ax^2 + bx - 48$ is a polynomial with three positive roots $p, q,$ and r such that $p < q < r$. What is the minimum possible value of $\dfrac{1}{p} + \dfrac{2}{q} + \dfrac{3}{r}$?

(A) $\dfrac{1}{2}$

(B) 1

(C) $\dfrac{3}{2}$

(D) 2

(E) $\dfrac{7}{2}$

04. If $a \geq b > 1$ what is the largest possible value of $\log_a(a/b) + \log_b(b/a)$?

(A) -2

(B) 0

(C) 2

(D) 3

(E) 4

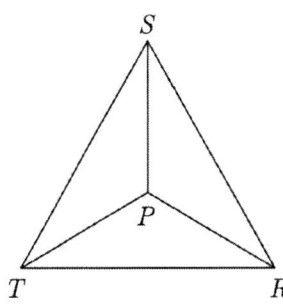

05. In the figure above, there is a point P inside the equilateral triangle STR with the length of each side is 8. The area of $\triangle SPT, \triangle TPR$, and $\triangle RPS$ is same. If the area of $\triangle SPT$ is A, $\triangle TPR$ is B, and $\triangle RPS$ is C, what is the minimum value of $A^2 + B^2 + C^2$?

(A) $16\sqrt{3}$

(B) 24

(C) $98\sqrt{3}$

(D) 256

(E) 312

06. What is the maximum value attained by $\dfrac{x^4 - x^2}{x^6 + 2x^3 - 1}$ over real numbers $x > 1$?

(A) $\dfrac{1}{6}$

(B) $\dfrac{1}{3}$

(C) $\dfrac{3}{2}$

(D) 2

(E) $\dfrac{5}{2}$

Chapter 6

➢ Binomial Theorem

The Binomial Theorem

AMC12에서 따로 출제되기 보다는 여러 단원에 걸쳐서 골고루 필요한 이론이다.
AIME의 경우 따로 출제되기도 한다.

본론으로 들어가 보자.

Pascal's Triangle

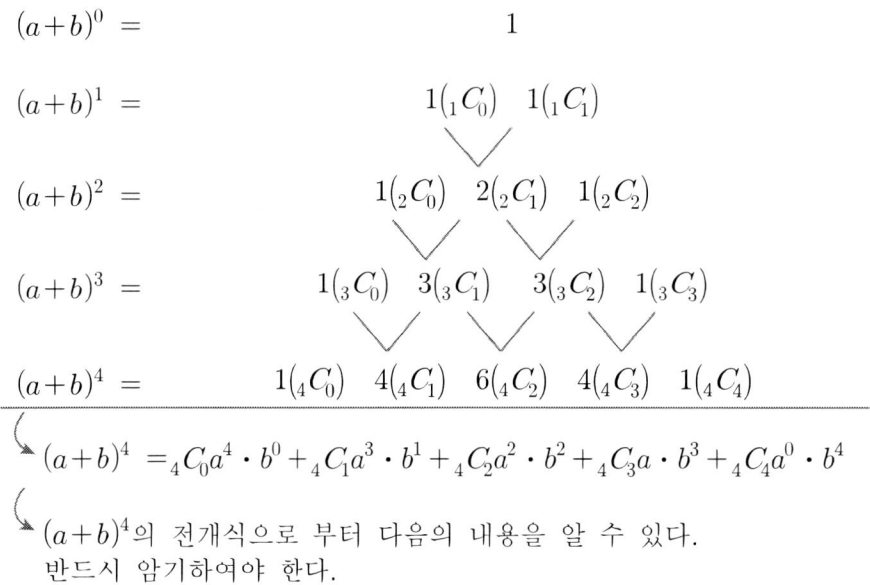

$$(a+b)^4 = {}_4C_0a^4 \cdot b^0 + {}_4C_1a^3 \cdot b^1 + {}_4C_2a^2 \cdot b^2 + {}_4C_3a \cdot b^3 + {}_4C_4a^0 \cdot b^4$$

$(a+b)^4$의 전개식으로 부터 다음의 내용을 알 수 있다.
반드시 암기하여야 한다.

①②를 암기하자!

① $(a+b)^n = {}_nC_0 \cdot a^n \cdot b^0 + {}_nC_1 \cdot a^{n-1} \cdot b^1 + {}_nC_2 \cdot a^{n-2} \cdot b^2 + \cdots + {}_nC_n \cdot a^0 \cdot b^n$

$a = 1,\ b = x$ 대입!

② $(1+x)^n = {}_nC_0 + {}_nC_1 \cdot x^1 + {}_nC_2 \cdot x^2 + \cdots + {}_nC_n \cdot x^n$

앞의 Pascal's Triangle을 보면...

1. Row를 모두 더하면 Coefficient의 총합이 된다.
2. $(a+b)^n$을 전개한 Coefficient들을 보면 대칭(Symmetry)이 된다.
    ⇐ ※ 앞으로 Equation 문제를 풀 때 상당히 중요한 내용이다.

다음을 보자.

$$(a+b)^3 = a^3 + ③a^2b + 3ab^2 + b^3$$

⇓

왜 a^2b는 Coefficient가 3인가?

⇒ a^2b는 $aab\ aba\ baa$이다.

즉, aab를 일렬로 배열하는 경우의 수 $= \dfrac{3!}{2!} = 3$

그렇다면, $(a+b+c)^6$ 에서 a^2b^3c의 Coefficient는?

⇒ $aabbbc$를 일렬로 배열하는 경우의 수!

$$\dfrac{6!}{2! \cdot 3!} = 60$$

$(a+b)^3$ 에서 Coefficient의 총합은 얼마인가?

(Solution) $(a+b)^3 = a^3 + 3a^2b + 3ab^2 + b^3$ 에서 $1+3+3+1=8$
이는 a,b 대신에 1을 대입한 결과와 같다.

※ 참고로 $(x-3y)^3 = x^3 + 3x^2(-3y) + 3x(-3y)^2 - 27y^3$
$= x^3 - 9x^2y + 27xy^2 - 27y^3$ 에서
Coefficient의 총합은 -8이고
이는 x, y 대신 1을 대입한 결과와 같다.

> · Coefficient의 총합은 변수(Variable) 대신 1을 대입!

다음의 예제들을 통해서 Coefficient를 어떻게 구하는지 알아보도록 하자.

(Example) Find the coefficient of $x^2 y^3$ for the expansion $(2x - 3y)^5$.

(Solution) 무조건 $(a+b)^n$ 꼴로 만든다!

① $a = 2x$, $b = -3y$ 라고 하면 $(a+b)^5$ 이 된다.

② $a^2 = (2x)^2$, $b^3 = (-3y)^3$ 에서 일단 $a^2 b^3$ 의 Coefficient를 찾는다.

③ $\underbrace{\underbrace{\dfrac{5!}{2!\,3!}}_{a^2 b^3 \text{의 coefficient}} \times 2^2 \times (-3)^3}_{x^2 y^3 \text{의 coefficient}} = -1080$

(Example) Find the coefficient of x^6 for the expansion $(3x^2 - 2)^5$.

(Solution) 무조건 $(a+b)^n$ 꼴로 만든다.

① $a = 3x^2$, $b = -2$ 라고 하면, $(a+b)^5$ 이 된다.

② $a^3 = (3x^2)^3$, $b^2 = (-2)^2$ 에서 일단 $a^3 b^2$ 의 Coefficient를 찾는다.

③ $\underbrace{\underbrace{\dfrac{5!}{3! \cdot 2!}}_{a^3 b^2 \text{의 coefficient}} \times 3^3 \times (-2)^2}_{x^6 \text{의 coefficient}} = 1080$

Coefficient 총합과 Coefficient의 활용

(Example) Coin을 네 번 던져서 Head 1번 Tail 3번 나올 Probability?

(Solution) 직접 세어 봐도 되지만 다음과 같이 해결 할 수 있다.

① $(H+T)^4$ 에서 Coefficient의 총합이 Number of Sample Space!
그러므로, $2^4 = 16$

② Head 1번, Tail 3번은 HT^3 의 Coefficient이고 Number of Event!
그러므로, $\dfrac{4!}{3!} = 4$

③ 그러므로, $P = \dfrac{4}{16} = \dfrac{1}{4}$

(Example) Dice를 세 번 던져서 3의 눈이 한 번, 4의 눈이 두 번 나올 Probability는?

(Solution) ① $1=a,\ 2=b,\ 3=c,\ 4=d,\ 5=e,\ 6=f$ 라고 하면,
$(a+b+c+d+e+f)^3$ 에서 Coefficient의 총합은 6^3.
그러므로, $n(S) = 6^3$

② cd^2 의 Coefficient는 $\dfrac{3!}{2!} = 3$

③ 그러므로, $P = \dfrac{3}{6^3} = \dfrac{1}{72}$

읽을거리

1. 큰 수와 작은 수

매우 큰 수를 읽는 데는 주로 중국과 인도에서 전래한 수사를 사용하는데 이것들이 오늘날 우리 것으로 토착화되었다.

(1) 큰 수 : 일, 십, 백, 천, 만, 억, 조, 경, 해, 자, 양, 구, 간, 정, 재, 극, 항하사, 아승기, 나유타, 불가사의, 무량대수(10⁶⁸)

(2) 작은 수 : 할, 푼, 리, 모, 사, 홀, 미, 섬, 사, 진, 애, 묘, 막, 모호, 준순, 수유, 순식, 탄지, 찰나, 육덕, 허공, 청정(10⁻²¹)

(3) 현대에 생겨난 수 : 광년, 매가톤, 미크론, 마이크로, 나노 등이 현대 과학의 발전상 필요에 의해서 새로이 생겨난 수사들이다.

2. 평행한 두 직선은 영원히 만나지 않는다

'평행한 두 직선은 영원히 만나지 않는다.' 라는 정리를 다시 한 번 생각해 보자.

우리가 자연을 유심히 살펴보면, 평행이란 관계 속에 있는 것이 수없이 많다. 고대 건축물인 파르테논 신전은 아폴로의 해변과 평행하게 만들어 하늘과 땅이 영원히 만나지 않는 신비로운 느낌을 주었다고 한다. 그러나 우리의 시각에 의하면, 평행한 두 직선은 만나고 있음을 알 수 있다. 평행한 길가의 가로수를 보면 저 먼 곳에서 한 점에서 만남을 볼 수 있다. 과연 이것이 착각일까, 아니면 실제로 만나는 것일까 궁금하다. 이러한 궁금증은 B.C 300년경의 유클리드(Euclid ; 330?~275? B. C.)가 평행선의 정리를 증명하지 못하고 공리로 인정함으로써 학문적으로 발생하였다.

유클리드의 공리는 '두 직선 m, n이 다른 직선 1과 교차할 때, 같은 쪽 내각의 합이 180°가 아니면 m, n은 같은 쪽 내각의 합이 180°보다 작은 쪽에서 만난다.'이다. 이것을 그림으로 나타내면 다음과 같다.

즉, $0° < a+b < 2 \angle R$이면, m, n의 교점은 a, b가 있는 쪽에 생긴다는 것이다.

그 후에 수많은 학자들이 이 평행선의 공리를 증명하기 위해 많은 시도를 하였으나 유한하고, 평면·공간적인 인간의 눈으로는 착각과 환상으로만 보이는 평행선의 신비를 증명할 수 없었다.

이러한 평행선의 신비 근처에는 '삼각형의 내각의 합이 180°보다 작거나 큰 새로운 공간이 있다.'는 상대성 이론에 의하여 우리가 살고 있는 공간은 평면 공간이 아닌 곡면, 타원적인 구면 공간임을 찾아 길가의 가로수가 먼 곳에서 만나는 것은 착각이 아닌 실제로 존재하고 있음을 알게 되었다.

Chapter 7

➢ Sequence & Recurrence Formula

Sequence

수들을 나열했을 때 일정한 규칙이 보이는 경우 이를 공식화시킨 단원이다.

Arithmetic Sequence와 Geometric Sequence의 증명은 이미 교과에서 많이 배운 내용이므로 생략하도록 하겠다.

중요한 것은 공식의 암기이다.

1. Arithmetic Sequence
$\Rightarrow a_n = a + (n-1)d$

$\Rightarrow S_n = \dfrac{n(a + a_n)}{2}$

　　(d : common difference, a : first term)

2. Geometric Sequence
$\Rightarrow a_n = ar^{n-1}$

$\Rightarrow S_n = \dfrac{a(1-r^n)}{1-r} = \dfrac{a(1-r^n)}{r-1}$

　　(r : common ratio, a : first term)

3. Infinite Geometric Series
$\Rightarrow$ Common Ratio를 r이라고 할 때, $-1 < r < 1$이면 $S = \dfrac{a}{1-r}$

　　(a : first term, r : common ratio)

$\Rightarrow$ 즉, $S = a + ar + ar^2 + \cdots = \dfrac{a}{1-r}$

4. Difference Sequence

한국에서는 계차수열이라고 배우고 미국의 교과 과정에서는 Difference가 Arithmetic Sequence가 되는 경우를 "Quadratic Model"이라고 배우는 단원이다.

다음의 두 가지 예를 보도록 하자.

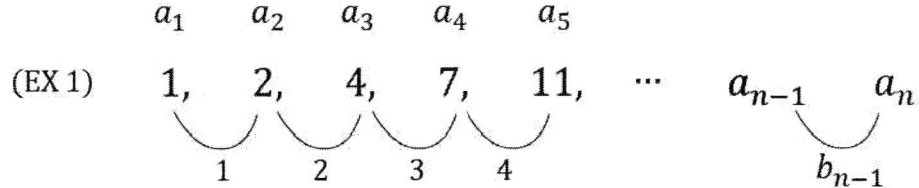

$\Rightarrow$ Difference가 Arithmetic Sequence

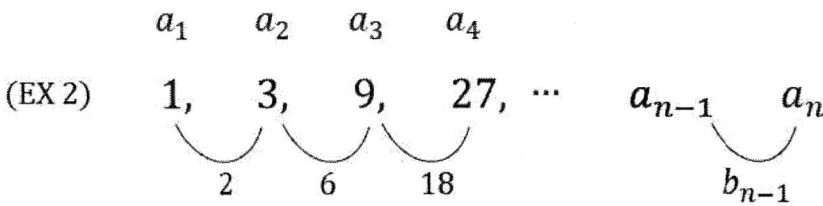

$\Rightarrow$ Difference가 Geometric Sequence

General Term을 다음과 같이 찾아보자.

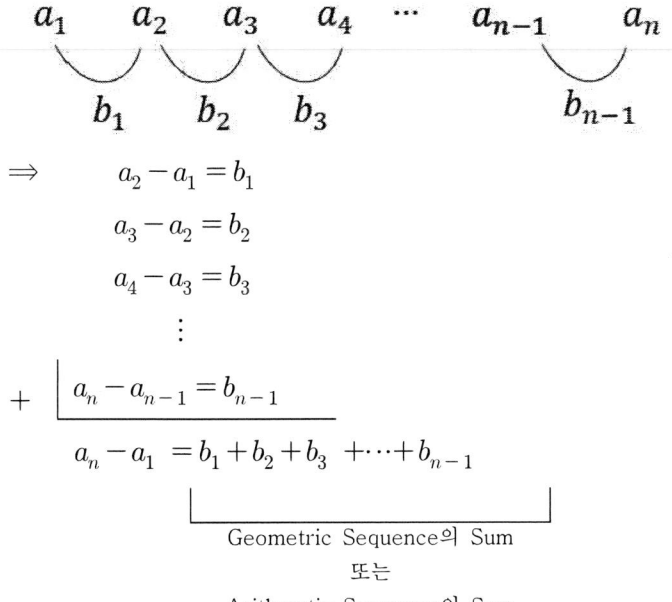

$\Rightarrow$
$$a_2 - a_1 = b_1$$
$$a_3 - a_2 = b_2$$
$$a_4 - a_3 = b_3$$
$$\vdots$$
$+$ $\underline{a_n - a_{n-1} = b_{n-1}}$
$$a_n - a_1 = b_1 + b_2 + b_3 + \cdots + b_{n-1}$$

Geometric Sequence의 Sum
또는
Arithmetic Sequence의 Sum

그러므로, $a_n = a + (b_1 + b_2 + b_3 + \cdots + b_{n-1})$의 공식이 성립하게 된다.

Recurrence Formula

한국 교과에서는 "점화식"이라고 배운다.

연속한 두 항(Term) 사이의 관계를 찾아내는 단원이다. 관계를 찾아내기 위해 우리는 n 대신 1, 2, 3, … 을 대입하여 Pattern을 찾아내게 된다.

다음의 예제를 보자.

(EX) If $a_{n+1} = a_n + 3$ and $a_1 = 1$, then a_{100}?

(Solution) $n = 1$일 때, $a_2 = a_1 + 3 = 4$ / $n = 2$일 때, $a_3 = a_2 + 3 = 7$ / $n = 3$일 때, $a_4 = a_3 + 3 = 10$...이고 Arithmetic Sequence이므로 $a_n = a + (n-1)d$

$\Rightarrow a_{100} = 1 + (100-1) \cdot 3 = 298$

간단한 예이지만 여기서 주목할 점은 Pattern을 찾았다는 점이다. 이 문제의 경우 간단하게 찾아지지만 대부분의 문제는 Pattern이 보일 때까지 끈기를 가지고 써 보아야 한다.

그렇다면, Pattern이 의미하는 것은 무엇일까?

Pattern이란 얼마마다 Repeat가 되는지... 어떤 Sequence Formula가 나오는지를 찾는 것인데 Pattern을 찾으려면 숫자를 다운시키면 보이게 된다. 숫자를 다운시킨다는 것은 문제를 통해서 익히도록 하자.

한국에서 공부한 학생들은 Recurrence Formula를 공식을 외워서 해결하려는 성향이 강한데 어느 공식을 찾으려고 노력하기 보다는 Pattern이 보일 때까지 직접 꾸준히 써 내려가는 연습을 하도록 하여야 한다.

01. A large equilateral triangle is constructed by using toothpicks to create rows of small equilateral triangles. For example, in the figure we have **3** rows of small congruent equilateral triangles, with **5** small triangles in the base row. How many toothpicks would be needed to construct a large equilateral triangle if the base row of the triangle consists of **2003** small equilateral triangles?

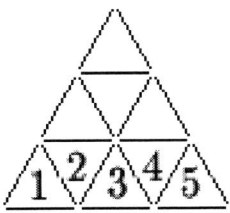

(A) 1,004,004

(B) 1,005,006

(C) 1,507,509

(D) 3,015,018

(E) 6,021,018

02. The first term of a sequence is 2005. Each succeeding term is the sum of the cubes of the digits of the previous terms. What is the 2005th term of the sequence?

(A) 29

(B) 55

(C) 85

(D) 133

(E) 250

03. The geometric series $a + ar + ar^2 + \cdots$ has a sum of 7, and the terms involving odd powers of r have a sum of 3. What is $a + r$?

(A) $\dfrac{4}{3}$

(B) $\dfrac{12}{7}$

(C) $\dfrac{3}{2}$

(D) $\dfrac{7}{3}$

(E) $\dfrac{5}{2}$

04. For each positive integer n, the mean of the first n terms of a sequence is n. What is the 2008th term of the sequence?

(A) 2008
(B) 4015
(C) 4016
(D) 4,030,056
(E) 4,032,064

05. The sequence S_1, S_2, S_3, $\cdots$, S_{10} has the property that every term beginning with the third is the sum of the previous two. That is, $S_n = S_{n-1} + S_{n-1}$ for $n \geq 3$. Suppose that $S_9 = 110$ and $S_7 = 42$. What is S_4?

(A) 4

(B) 6

(C) 10

(D) 12

(E) 16

06. Let $a + ar_1 + ar_1^2 + ar_1^3 \cdots$ and $a + ar_2 + ar_2^2 + ar_2^3 + \cdots$ be two different infinite geometric series of positive numbers with the same first term. The sum of the first series is r_1, and the sum of the second series is r_2. What is $r_1 + r_2$?

(A) 0

(B) $\dfrac{1}{2}$

(C) 1

(D) $\dfrac{1 + \sqrt{5}}{2}$

(E) 2

07. Let $a < b < c$ be three integers such that a, b, c is an arithmetic progression and a, c, b is a geometric progression. What is the smallest possible value of c

(A) -2

(B) 1

(C) 2

(D) 4

(E) 6

08. Let a_1, a_2, $\cdots$, a_k be a finite arithmetic sequence with $a_4 + a_7 + a_{10} = 17$ and $a_4 + a_5 + \cdots + a_{13} + a_{14} = 77$. If $a_k = 13$, then $k =$

(A) 16

(B) 18

(C) 20

(D) 22

(E) 24

09. For a finite sequence $A = (a_1, a_2, \cdots, a_n)$ of numbers, the *Cesaro sum* of A is defined to be $\dfrac{S_1 + \cdots + S_n}{n}$, where $S_k = a_1 + \cdots + a_k$ and $1 \le k \le n$. If the Cesaro sum of the 99-term sequence $(a_1, \cdots, a_{99})$ is 1000, what is the Cesaro sum of the 100-term sequence $(1, a_1, \cdots, a_{99})$?

(A) 991

(B) 999

(C) 1000

(D) 1001

(E) 1009

10. The *Fibonacci numbers* are defined recursively by the equation

$$F_n = F_{n-1} + F_{n-2}$$

for every integer $n \ge 2$, with initial values $F_0 = 0$ and $F_1 = 1$. Let $G_n = F - 3n$ be every third Fibonacci number. There are constants a and b such that every integer $n \ge 2$ satisfies

$$G_n = aG_{n-1} + bG_{n-2}.$$

What is the ordered pair (a, b)?

(A) (4, 1)

(B) (4, 2)

(C) (3, 1)

(D) (3, 2)

(E) (3, 3)

11. The three roots of the cubic $30x^3 - 50x^2 + 22x - 1$ are distinct real numbers between 0 and 1. For every non-negative integer n, let s_n be the sum of the nth powers of these three roots. What is the value of the infinite series

$$s_0 + s_1 + s_2 + s_3 + \cdots ?$$

(A) 10

(B) 12

(C) 14

(D) 16

(E) 18

12. The sequence $a_0,\ a_1,\ a_2,\ \cdots$ satisfies the recurrence equation

$$a_n = 2a_{n-1} - 2a_{n-2} + a_{n-3}$$

for every integer $n \geq 3$. If $a_{20} = 1$, $a_{25} = 10$, and $a_{30} = 100$, what is the value of a_{1331}?

(A) 170

(B) 174

(C) 175

(D) 181

(E) 182

13. Define a sequence of real numbers a_1, a_2, a_3, $\cdots$ by $a_1 = 1$ and $a_{n+1}^3 = 99a_n^3$ for all $n \geq 1$. Then a_{100} equals :

   (A) 33^{33}

   (B) 33^{99}

   (C) 99^{33}

   (D) 99^{99}

   (E) none of these

14. The sequence a_1, a_2, a_3, $\cdots$ satisfies $a_1 = 19$, $a_9 = 99$, and, for all $n \geq 3$, a_n is the arithmetic mean of the first $n-1$ terms. What is the value of a_2?

   (A) 176

   (B) 177

   (C) 178

   (D) 179

   (E) 180

15. The sequence 1, 2, 1, 2, 2, 1, 2, 2, 2, 1, 2, 2, 2, 2, 1, 2, 2, 2, 2, 2, 1, 2, ⋯ consists of 1's separated by blocks of 2's with n 2's in the nth block. The sum of the first 1234 terms of this sequence is

    (A) 1996

    (B) 2419

    (C) 2429

    (D) 2439

    (E) 2449

16. Consider the triangular array of numbers with 0, 1, 2, 3, ⋯ along the sides and interior numbers obtained by adding the two adjacent numbers in the previous row. Rows 1 through 6 are shown.

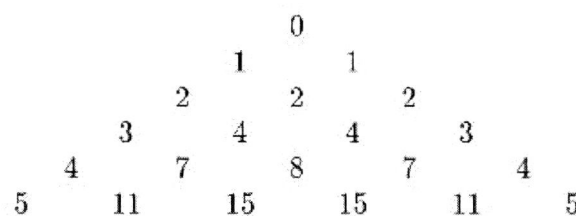

Let $f(n)$ denote the sum of the numbers in row n. What is the remainder when $f(100)$ is divided by 100?

    (A) 12

    (B) 30

    (C) 50

    (D) 62

    (E) 74

Chapter 8

➢ **Counting & Probability**

Counting

"경우의 수"를 구하는 것인데 이 부분을 어렵다고 느끼는 이유는 문제를 접하는 순간부터 $_nC_r$ or $_nP_r$ 부터 떠올리기 때문이다. $_nC_r$ or $_nP_r$ 과 같은 도구들은 빨리 풀기위한 도구일 뿐이다.

초등학교 때 Sum을 배우고 나서 Product를 배운다.
그 이유는 이렇다.

❶ 2를 세 번 더해보자.
  $\Rightarrow 2+2+2=6$
❷ 2가 세 번 반복되므로 빨리 계산하기 위해서 곱하기를 한다.
  $\Rightarrow 2\times3=6$

즉, Sum을 빨리 하기 위해서 Product를 하는 것이다.
그렇다면 Sum을 모르고 Product를 알 수 있을까? 이는 Counting문제를 접하는 순간부터 $_nC_r$ or $_nP_r$ 부터 떠올리는 것과 같은 것이다. 왜냐하면, $_nC_r$ 이나 $_nP_r$ 모두 Product를 빨리 계산하기 위한 도구들이기 때문이다.

결론을 말하자면, Counting문제는 모두 Sum으로 풀리는 것이다. Sum으로 풀다보면 Product 가 보이고 $_nC_r$ 이나 $_nP_r$ 이 보이는 것이다.

다음을 보자.

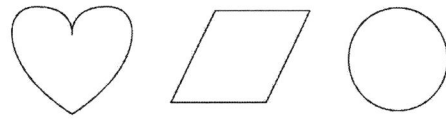

위 그림에서 서로 다른 그림의 개수는?
$1+1+1=3$. 즉, 하나씩 일일이 세어봐서 더하는 것이 바로 Sum이다!

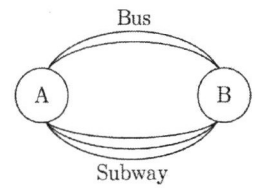

위의 그림에서 A지역에서 B지역으로 가는 방법은 모두 몇 가지인가?
⇒ Bus(2)+Subway(3)＝5가지

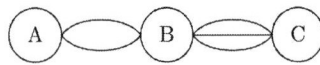

위의 그림에서 A에서 B를 거쳐서 C까지 가는 방법은 모두 몇 가지인가?

❶ 대부분의 학생들은 $2 \times 3 = 6$이라고 답한다.

❷ 하지만 다음의 풀이가 본래의 풀이 방법이다.

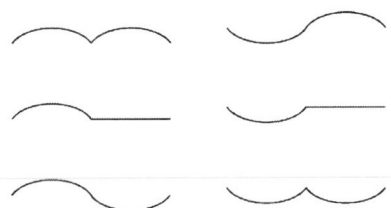

이와 같이 일일이 세어보면 6가지

이를 좀 더 빨리 계산해보면
서로 다른 두 가지 (◯)에 대해
세 가지 (◯)가 반복되고 있으므로 $2 \times 3 = 6$

다음의 경우를 보자.

2, 3, 4를 이용하여 만들 수 있는 Positive three digit even integer(세 자리 짝수)는 몇 가지인가?

❶ Sum의 방법을 이용하자! 즉, Case by Case!
(Case 1)　　2 3 4
(Case 2)　　3 2 4
(Case 3)　　3 4 2
(Case 4)　　4 3 2
총 4가지 Case가 나온다.

❷ 좀 더 빨리 계산하기 위해 Product 방법을 이용한다.
Product 방법을 이용하기에 애매한 경우를 나눈다.

Even integer는 Unit digit이 Even digit 이므로 다음과 같이 분류시킨다.

(Case 1)　　↑　　　↑　　　2
　　　　　　2가지 × 1가지 = 2가지

(Case 2)　　↑　　　↑　　　4
　　　　　　2가지 × 1가지 = 2가지

그러므로 총 4가지.

Sum의 방법으로 4가지 Case가 나오지만 Product의 방법을 사용하게 되면 Case가 두 가지로 줄어든다.

실제로 Case를 분류시키는 것은 상당히 중요하다.

다음의 경우를 보자.

0, 1, 2, 3을 이용하여 만들 수 있는 Positive four digit even integer는 몇 가지인가?

❶ Sum의 방법을 이용하자! Case by Case!

(Case 1)	1 2 3 0	(Case 6)	3 2 1 0
(Case 2)	1 3 2 0	(Case 7)	1 0 3 2
(Case 3)	2 1 3 0	(Case 8)	1 3 0 2
(Case 4)	2 3 1 0	(Case 9)	3 1 0 2
(Case 5)	3 1 2 0	(Case 10)	3 0 1 2

총 10가지가 나온다!

❷ Sum의 방법이 익숙하다면 Product의 방법을 이용한다!
다음과 같이 Unit digit의 0과 2인 경우로 분류한다.

(Case 1)   ↑   ↑   ↑ $\boxed{0}$
3가지 × 2가지 × 1가지 = 6가지

(Case 2)   ↑   ↑   ↑ $\boxed{2}$
0을   × 2가지 × 1가지 = 4가지
제외한
2가지

그러므로 총 6+4=10가지.

Product를 빨리하기 위한 도구 $n!$

· $n! = n \times (n-1) \times (n-2) \times \cdots \times 3 \times 2 \times 1$

다음의 간단한 경우의 예를 보도록 하자.

a, b, c를 일렬로 배열하는 방법의 수는?

❶ Sum의 방법을 이용!

abc   bac   cab
acb   bca   cba

총 6가지 Case가 나온다.

❷ Product 방법을 이용!

3가지 $\times$ 2가지 $\times$ 1가지 $=$ 6가지

❸ $n!$ 이용

$3! = 6$가지

위의 경우에서 보는 것처럼 ① Sum의 방법이 익숙해지면 ② Product의 방법을 이용하고 Product의 방법이 익숙해지면 ③ $n!$ $_nC_r$ $_nP_r$ ... 와 같은 도구를 사용한다.

고난이도 문제일수록 처음부터 $n!$ $_nC_r$ $_nP_r$ 와 같은 도구를 사용하려면 잘 해결이 안 된다. Sum의 방법으로 풀다보면 Product의 방법이 보이고 $n!$ $_nC_r$ $_nP_r$ 와 같은 도구의 쓰임이 보이는 것이다.

Counting문제를 풀 때, 우선 Sum의 방법을 쓴다는 것은 Case를 분류시키는 것이다. 분류가 잘 되고 나면 Product 방법이나 $n!$ $_nC_r$ $_nP_r$ 와 같은 도구의 쓰임이 잘 보이게 된다.

$$_nP_r \quad _nC_r \quad _nH_r$$

❶ $_nP_r$: 7개 중 r개를 일렬로 배열 (Permutation)

$$n! = \underbrace{\overset{\text{1st}}{n} \times \overset{\text{2nd}}{(n-1)} \times \overset{\text{3rd}}{(n-2)} \times \cdots \times \overset{r\text{th}}{(n-(r-1))}}_{nPr} \times \underbrace{\overset{(r+1)\text{th}}{(n-r)} \times \cdots 3 \times 2 \times 1}_{(n-r)!}$$

그러므로, $nPr = \dfrac{n!}{(n-r)!}$

(Example)

$\cdot \ _5P_3 = \dfrac{5!}{(5-3)!} = 5 \cdot 4 \cdot 3$ $\qquad\qquad \cdot \ _6P_2 = \dfrac{6!}{(6-2)!} = 6 \cdot 5$

$\cdot \ _4P_2 = \dfrac{4!}{(4-2)!} = 4 \cdot 3$ $\qquad\qquad \cdot \ _2P_2 = \dfrac{2!}{(2-2)!} = 2!$

$\qquad\qquad\qquad\qquad\qquad\qquad\qquad (※ \ 0! = 1)$

❷ $_nC_r$: n중 r개를 순서 없이 뽑기 (Combination) (즉, random하게 뽑기)

$\cdot$ $\underbrace{n\text{개 중 } r\text{개 일렬배열}}_{nPr} = \underbrace{n\text{개 중 } r\text{개 뽑고}}_{nCr} \underbrace{r\text{개 일렬배열}}_{r!}$

$\qquad\qquad nPr \qquad = \qquad nCr \qquad \times \qquad r!$

그러므로 $_nC_r = \dfrac{_nP_r}{r!}$ 에서 $_nP_r = \dfrac{n!}{(n-r)!}$ 이므로

$$_nC_r = \dfrac{n!}{r!(n-r)!}$$

(Example) $\cdot \ _5C_2 = \dfrac{5!}{2!(5-2)!} = \dfrac{5 \cdot 4}{2 \cdot 1}$ $\qquad\qquad \cdot \ _5C_3 = \dfrac{5!}{3!(5-3)!} = \dfrac{5 \cdot 4 \cdot 3}{3 \cdot 2 \cdot 1}$

❸ $_nH_r$: n개 중 r개를 중복해서 순서 없이 뽑기
　　　　　(Homogeneous Combination)

다음의 예를 보자.

A, B, C 중에 중복을 허용하여 두 개를 뽑는다고 해 보자.

⇒ AA, BB, CC, AB, AC, BC . . . 총 6가지

즉, $_3H_2 = 6$인 것인데 이는 $_4C_2$ 와 결과가 같다.
$_3H_2 = {_4C_2}$ 이므로 $_3H_2 = {_{(3+2)-1}C_2}$.

그러므로 $_nH_r = {_{(n+r)-1}C_r}$

(Example) · $_4H_2 = {_{(4+2)-1}C_2} = {_5C_2} = \dfrac{5 \cdot 4}{2 \cdot 1} = 10$

　　　　　 · $_2H_3 = {_{(2+3)-1}C_3} = {_4C_3} = \dfrac{4 \cdot 3 \cdot 2}{3 \cdot 2 \cdot 1} = 4$

$_nP_r$ 　 $_nC_r$ 　 $_nH_r$ 에서 n은 선택할 수 있는 대상 r은 선택의 개수이다.
$_nP_r$ 과 $_nC_r$은 모두 $n \geq r$ 이어야 하지만 $_nH_r$ 은 중복선택이 가능하기 때문에
$n < r$이 될 수도 있다.

A, B, C를 일렬로 배열하는 경우를 생각 해 보자.

❶ Sum의 방법을 이용하면

   ABC   BAC   ACB   BCA   CAB   CBA … 총 6가지

❷ $n!$을 이용하면 $3! = 6$

여기에서 B대신 A를 대입하면

AAC   AAC   ACA   ACA   CAA   CAA … 총 3가지

즉, AAC를 배열하는 방법은 3가지로 줄어든다.
B대신 A를 대입하면서 AB BA 두 가지가 AA 한 가지로 줄어들기 때문이다.
그러므로 AAC를 일렬로 배열하는 경우의 수는 $\dfrac{3!}{2!} = 3$.

예를 들어, AAABCC를 일렬로 배열하는 경우의 수는 $\dfrac{6!}{3! \cdot 2!}$ 이 된다.

다음의 경우를 보자.

(Example) 3개 중 2개 뽑기

❶ $_nC_r$ 이용! $\Rightarrow {}_3C_2 = 3$

❷ Sum 이용

A	B	C
○	○	×
○	×	○
×	○	○

                … 3가지

❸ 3개 중 2개를 뽑기 때문에 ○ 2개×1개를 배열하는 경우의 수 $= \dfrac{3!}{2!} = 3$

즉, 군이 $_nC_r$을 사용하지 않아도 Sum의 방법으로도 구할 수 있는 것이다.

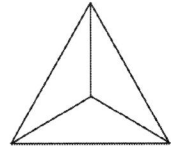

(Example) 위의 그림처럼 세 개의 삼각형에 두 가지 Color인 Blue, Red를 중복해서 칠할
수 있는 경우의 수는?

(Solution 1) 직접 세어본다. (Sum)

(B, B, B), (R, R, R), (R, R, B), (R, B, B) ⋯ 4가지

(Solution 2) 선택 할 수 있는 대상은 Blue, Red 두 개인데 세 개를 선택해야 한다.
즉, 선택할 수 있는 대상보다 선택이 많은 경우 쓸 수 있는 것은 $_nH_r$!
그러므로 $_2H_3 = {}_{(2+3)-1}C_3 = {}_4C_3 = 4$.

Counting 문제를 풀 때...

1. 무조건 $_nP_r$, $_nC_r$, $_nH_r$ 에만 의존하려고 하지 말고

2. Sum의 방법으로 풀다가 (Case by Case)보면 빨리 푸는 방향이 보인다.
이 때, 분류를 잘 해야 한다.

3. 빨리 푸는 방향이 보일 때, $_nP_r$, $_nC_r$, $_nH_r$ 등과 같은 도구를 이용한다.
어차피 $_nP_r$, $_nC_r$, $_nH_r$ 도 모두 Sum의 방법으로 풀리는 것 들이다.

Probability

$$\text{Probability of Event} = \frac{\text{Nmber of Event}}{\text{Nmber of Sample Space}}$$

이를 줄여서 표현하면

$$P(E) = \frac{n(E)}{n(S)}$$

Probability는 다음과 같은 성질을 갖는다.

❶ $0 \leq P(E) \leq 1$

아무리 작아봐야 0이고 커봐야 1이다.

즉, Probability의 가장 큰 값이 1이므로

$P^c = 1 - P$라는 사실을 알 수 있다.

❷ $n(A \cup B) = n(A) + n(B) - n(AnB)$ 의 양변을 $n(S)$ 로 나누면,

$$\frac{n(A \cup B)}{n(S)} = \frac{n(A)}{n(S)} + \frac{n(B)}{n(S)} - \frac{n(AnB)}{n(S)}$$

즉, $P(A \cup B) = P(A) + P(B) - P(AnB)$

Probability 문제를 잘 풀기 위해서는 기초적인 원리부터 이해를 하여야 한다.
AMC 또는 AIME에 나오는 고난이도 문제들도 모두 기초적인 원리를 이용해도 해결이 되기 때문이다.

특히 하나하나 분리 (Case by Case)하는 연습이 매우 중요하다.

언제 더하고 곱하는가?

보통 "and" 이면 곱하고 "or" 이면 더하는 것으로 알고 있다.
맞는 말이지만 이렇게 막연하게만 알고 있으면 고난이도 문제를 해결하는데 어려울 수 있다.

다음의 경우를 보자.

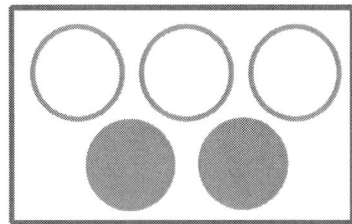

위의 그림처럼 Box안에 흰 공 3개, 검은 공 2개가 있다고 해 보자.
여기에서 흰 공 1개를 뽑고 검은 공 1개를 뽑는 경우의 Probability를 구해보도록 하자.

1. 다음과 같이 간단하게 구할 수 있다.

$$P = \frac{3}{5} \times \frac{2}{4} = \frac{6}{20} = \frac{3}{10}$$

2. 위의 1에서는 간단하게 곱해서 풀었는데 그 이유를 자세히 살펴보자.

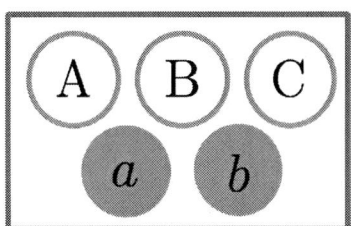

· $n(S)$

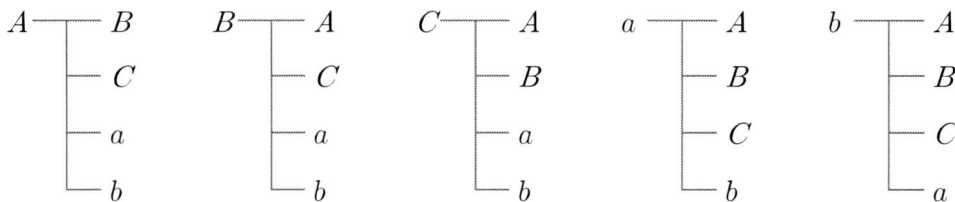

그러므로, $n(S)$는 모든 경우를 더해보면 20가지이다.

2를 3번 더하면 6이 되는데 이를 빨리 계산하기 위해 $2 \times 3 = 6$ 처럼 곱하기를 한다.
이 경우에도 서로 다른 다섯 가지 경우에 각각 네 가지가 반복되기 때문에 5×4를 하는 것이다.

· $n(E)$
  흰 공 1개를 뽑고 검은 공 1개를 뽑는 경우.

$$A \begin{cases} a \\ b \end{cases} \qquad B \begin{cases} a \\ b \end{cases} \qquad C \begin{cases} a \\ b \end{cases}$$

그러므로, $n(E)$는 모든 경우를 더해보면 6가지이다.
서로 다른 세 가지 경우에 각각 두 가지가 반복되므로 $3 \times 2 = 6$

그러므로, $P(E) = \dfrac{n(E)}{n(S)} = \dfrac{6}{20} = \dfrac{3}{10}$

위의 문제에서 일일이 모든 경우를 세는 경우가 더하기 방법이다. (Case by Case)
이를 빨리 계산하기 위해 곱하기 방법을 쓰는 것이다.

고난이도 문제일수록 한 번에 곱하기 방법을 쓰려면 문제의 해결 방향이 잘 안 보이게 된다.
그러므로, 고난이도 문제일수록 더하기 (Case by Case)를 잘 해야 한다.
더하기가 숙달되면 곱하기가 잘 보이게 된다.

다음의 경우를 보자.

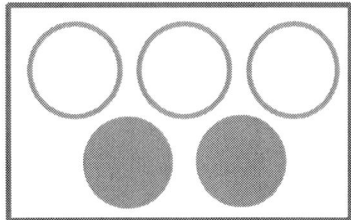

위의 그림처럼 Box안에 흰 공 3개와 검은 공 2개가 있다고 해 보자. 먼저 Sally가 공 하나를 뽑은 다음 Andy가 검은 공을 뽑을 확률을 구해보자.

다음과 같이 두 가지 Case로 나누어 생각한다.

❶ Sally가 흰 공을 뽑는 경우

❷ Sally가 검은 공을 뽑는 경우

이처럼 두 가지 Case로 나누어 생각하는 이유는 Sally가 흰 공을 뽑는지 검은 공을 뽑는지에 따라서 Andy가 검은 공을 뽑을 확률이 달라지기 때문이다.

Case 1. Sally가 흰 공을 뽑고 Andy가 검은 공을 뽑는 경우

$$\boxed{\frac{3}{5} \times \frac{2}{4}} = \frac{6}{20}$$

    ※ Case by Case로 구해도 된다.
       원래는 더하기로 구하는 것인데 곱하기 방법으로 빨리 구하는 것이다.

Case 2. Sally가 검은 공을 뽑고 Andy가 검은 공을 뽑는 경우

$$\frac{2}{5} \times \frac{1}{4} = \frac{2}{20}$$

그러므로 Case 1 + Case 2 $= \frac{8}{20} = \frac{2}{5}$

이 문제에서 원래는 모든 경우를 분류해서 더해서 풀면 되지만 계산을 빨리하기 위해서 곱하기 방법과 더하기 방법을 같이 사용하였다.

이 문제를 통해서 이렇게 알아두도록 하자!

 모든 Probability 문제들은 모든 경우를 분류해서 더해서 구해야 하지만 계산 편의를 위해 곱하기를 쓸 수 있는 부분은 곱하기를 사용한다. 즉, 곱하기를 쓰기가 애매한 경우들을 먼저 분류하고 각각의 경우들을 곱하기로 구한 다음 더하면 되는 것이다!

이를 정리해 보면,

Probability 문제는

---

1. 각각의 경우를 분류

2. 각 경우를 곱하기로 구하고

3. 각각의 경우를 더한다.

독립 시행의 확률

같은 행동을 여러 번 반복하는 경우 공식을 이용하여 구할 수 있다.

다음을 보자.

주사위를 3번 던져서 1의 눈이 한 번 나올 확률을 구해보자.

(Solution 1)

	1회	2회	3회
Case 1	○	×	×

$$\frac{1}{6} \times \left(1-\frac{1}{6}\right) \times \left(1-\frac{1}{6}\right) = \left(\frac{1}{6}\right)^1\left(1-\frac{1}{6}\right)^{3-1}$$

Case 2	×	○	×

$$\left(1-\frac{1}{6}\right) \times \frac{1}{6} \times \left(1-\frac{1}{6}\right) = \left(\frac{1}{6}\right)^1\left(1-\frac{1}{6}\right)^{3-1}$$

Case 3	×	×	○

$$\left(1-\frac{1}{6}\right)\times\left(1-\frac{1}{6}\right) \times \frac{1}{6} = \left(\frac{1}{6}\right)^1\left(1-\frac{1}{6}\right)^{3-1}$$

그러므로 Case 1 + Case 2 + Case 3

$$= 3 \cdot \left(\frac{1}{6}\right)^1 \cdot \left(1-\frac{1}{6}\right)^{3-1}$$

계산 결과를 자세히 분석해보면...

$\boxed{3}$ × $\boxed{\dfrac{1}{6}}$ ① 실행된 횟수 × $\boxed{1-\dfrac{1}{6}}$ ③-1 실행이 안 된 횟수

⇓   ⇓   ⇓

Case가 3가지   실행된 확률(P)   실행이 안 된 확률 $(1-P)$

⇓

○ · × · ×를 일렬로 배열 하는 경우의 수 $= {}_3C_1$

그러므로, 다음과 같이 결론을 내릴 수 있다.

같은 행동을 n번 반복하여 r번 실행 된 확률

$$P = {}_nC_r \cdot P^r \cdot (1-P)^{n-r}$$

다음의 간단한 경우도 보도록 하자.
너무나 당연한 것이지만 고난이도 문제에서 이와 같은 간단한 개념들도 활용이 된다.

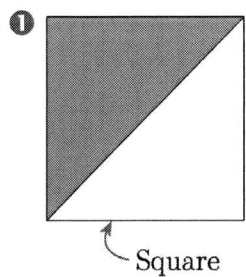

색칠 된 부분이 차지하는 비율 $= \dfrac{1}{2}$

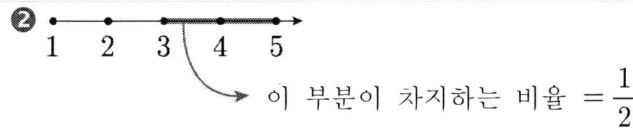

이 부분이 차지하는 비율 $= \dfrac{1}{2}$

01. How many 2−person committee can be formed from a group of 4?

    (A) 2

    (B) 3

    (C) 4

    (D) 6

    (E) 12

02. A committee of 3 men and 2 women is being selected from a group of 5 men and 4 women. How many different committees are possible?

    (A) 24

    (B) 32

    (C) 48

    (D) 60

    (E) 120

Color 1	Color 2	Color 1

03. As shown above, a certain design is to be painted using 2 different colors. If 4 different colors are available for the design, how many differently painted designs are possible?

(A) 6
(B) 8
(C) 12
(D) 16
(E) 24

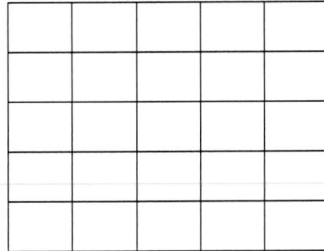

04. As the picture above shows, a paper board is divided into 25 squares. Andy writes A and Benton writes B in one squares each. If Andy does not write on either the same row or column as Benton, how many different ways are possible to write A and B on 25 squares?

(A) 60
(B) 80
(C) 120
(D) 320
(E) 400

05. In a class, 3 students play the violin and 4 students play the piano. How many possibilities are there to combine 1 piano player with two violin players for a recital?

    (A) 6

    (B) 8

    (C) 12

    (D) 16

    (E) 24

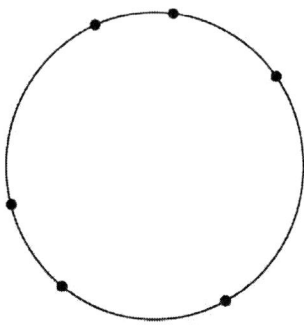

06. As shown in the figure above, there are 6 different points on a circle. How many triangles with different vertex can be formed?

    (A) 6

    (B) 12

    (C) 15

    (D) 20

    (E) 24

07. Pat wants to buy four doughnuts from an ample supply of three types of doughnuts: glazed, chocolate, and powdered. How many different selections are possible?

    (A) 6

    (B) 9

    (C) 12

    (D) 15

    (E) 18

08. Pat is to select six cookies from a tray containing only chocolate chip, oatmeal, and peanut butter cookies. There are at least six of each of these three kinds of cookies on the tray. How many different assortments of six cookies can be selected?

    (A) 22

    (B) 25

    (C) 27

    (D) 28

    (E) 729

09. Each face of a regular tetrahedron is painted either red, white or blue. Two colorings are considered indistinguishable if two congruent tetrahedra with those colorings can be rotated so that their appearances are identical. How many distinguishable colorings are possible?

(A) 15
(B) 18
(C) 27
(D) 54
(E) 81

10. At a twins and triplets convention, there were 9 sets of twins and 6 sets of triplets, all from different families. Each twin shook hands with all the twins except his/her siblings and with half the triplets. Each triplet shook hands with all the triplets except his/her siblings and with half the twins. How many handshakes took place?

(A) 324
(B) 441
(C) 630
(D) 648
(E) 882

118

11. Bob and Alice each have a bag that contains one ball of each of the colors blue, green, orange, red, and violet. Alice randomly selects one ball from her bag and puts it into Bob's bag. Bob then randomly selects one ball from his bag and puts it into Alice's bag. What is the probability that after this process, the contents of the two bags are the same?

(A) $\dfrac{1}{10}$

(B) $\dfrac{1}{6}$

(C) $\dfrac{1}{5}$

(D) $\dfrac{1}{3}$

(E) $\dfrac{1}{2}$

12. Coin A is flipped three times and coin B is flipped four times. What is the probability that the number of heads obtained from flipping the two fair coins is the same?

(A) $\dfrac{29}{128}$

(B) $\dfrac{23}{128}$

(C) $\dfrac{1}{4}$

(D) $\dfrac{35}{128}$

(E) $\dfrac{1}{2}$

13. Twelve fair dice are rolled. What is the probability that the product of the numbers on the top faces is prime?

(A) $(\frac{1}{12})^{12}$

(B) $(\frac{1}{6})^{12}$

(C) $2(\frac{1}{6})^{11}$

(D) $\frac{5}{2}(\frac{1}{6})^{11}$

(E) $(\frac{1}{6})^{10}$

14. What is the probability that an integer in the set $\{1, 2, 3, \cdots, 100\}$ is divisible by 2 and not divisible by 3?

(A) $\frac{1}{6}$

(B) $\frac{33}{100}$

(C) $\frac{17}{50}$

(D) $\frac{1}{2}$

(E) $\frac{18}{25}$

15. The wheel shown is spun twice, and the randomly determined numbers opposite the pointer are recorded. The first number is divided by 4, and the second number is divided by 5. The first remainder designates a column, and the second remainder designates a row on the checkerboard shown. What is the probability that the pair of numbers designates a shaded square?

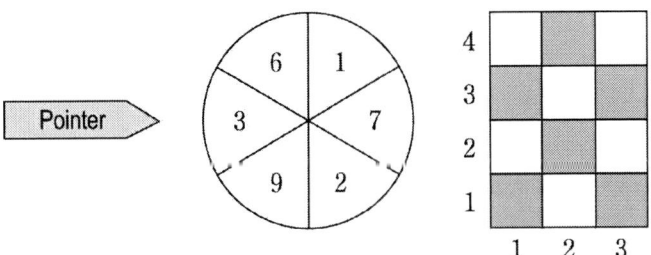

(A) $\dfrac{1}{3}$

(B) $\dfrac{4}{9}$

(C) $\dfrac{1}{2}$

(D) $\dfrac{5}{9}$

(E) $\dfrac{2}{3}$

16. Tina randomly selects two distinct numbers from the set $\{1, 2, 3, 4, 5\}$, and Sergio randomly selects a number from the set $\{1, 2, \cdots, 10\}$. What is the probability that Sergio's number is larger than the sum of the two numbers chosen by Tina?

   (A) $2/5$
   (B) $9/20$
   (C) $1/2$
   (D) $11/20$
   (E) $24/25$

17. Three distinct vertices of a cube are chosen at random. What is the probability that the plane determined by these three vertices contains points inside the cube?

   (A) $\dfrac{1}{4}$

   (B) $\dfrac{3}{8}$

   (C) $\dfrac{4}{7}$

   (D) $\dfrac{5}{7}$

   (E) $\dfrac{3}{4}$

18. A coin is altered so that the probability that it lands on heads is less than $\frac{1}{2}$ and when the coin is flipped four times, the probability of an equal number of heads and tails is $\frac{1}{6}$. What is the probability that the coin lands on heads?

(A) $\dfrac{\sqrt{15}-3}{6}$

(B) $\dfrac{(6-\sqrt{6})(\sqrt{6}+2)}{12}$

(C) $\dfrac{\sqrt{2}-1}{2}$

(D) $\dfrac{3-\sqrt{3}}{6}$

(E) $\dfrac{\sqrt{3}-1}{2}$

19. Consider a fair coin and a fair 6−sided die. The die begins with the number 1 face up. A step starts with a toss of the coin: if the coin comes out heads, we roll the die; otherwise (if the coin comes out tails), we do nothing else in this step. After 5 such steps, what is the probability that the number 1 is face up on the die?

(A) $\dfrac{1}{4}$

(B) $\dfrac{5}{8}$

(C) $\dfrac{43}{79}$

(D) $\dfrac{53}{107}$

(E) $\dfrac{37}{192}$

20. One fair die has faces 1, 1, 2, 2, 3, 3 and another has faces 4, 4, 5, 5, 6, 6. The dice are rolled and the numbers on the top faces are added. What is the probability that the sum will be odd?

(A) $\dfrac{1}{3}$

(B) $\dfrac{4}{9}$

(C) $\dfrac{1}{2}$

(D) $\dfrac{5}{9}$

(E) $\dfrac{2}{3}$

21. A pair of standard 6−sided dice fair dice is rolled once. The sum of the numbers rolled determines the diameter of a circle. What is the probability that the numerical value of the area of the circle is less than the numerical value of the circle's circumference?

(A) $\dfrac{1}{36}$

(B) $\dfrac{1}{12}$

(C) $\dfrac{1}{6}$

(D) $\dfrac{1}{4}$

(E) $\dfrac{5}{18}$

22. Juan rolls a fair regular octahedral die marked with the numbers 1 through 8. Then Amal rolls a fair six-sided die. What is the probability that the product of the two rolls is a multiple of 3?

(A) $\dfrac{1}{12}$

(B) $\dfrac{1}{3}$

(C) $\dfrac{1}{2}$

(D) $\dfrac{7}{12}$

(E) $\dfrac{2}{3}$

23. For a particular peculiar pair of dice, the probabilities of rolling 1, 2, 3, 4, 5 and 6 on each die are in the ratio $1:2:3:4:5:6$. What is the probability of rolling a total of 7 on the two dice?

(A) $\dfrac{4}{63}$

(B) $\dfrac{1}{8}$

(C) $\dfrac{8}{63}$

(D) $\dfrac{1}{6}$

(E) $\dfrac{2}{7}$

24. Two eight-sided dice each have faces numbered 1 through 8. When the dice are rolled, each face has an equal probability of appearing on the top. What is the probability that the product of the two top numbers is greater than their sum?

(A) $\dfrac{1}{2}$

(B) $\dfrac{47}{64}$

(C) $\dfrac{3}{4}$

(D) $\dfrac{55}{64}$

(E) $\dfrac{7}{8}$

25. Jacob uses the following procedure to write down a sequence of numbers. First he chooses the first term to be 6. To generate each succeeding term, he flips a fair coin. If it comes up heads, he doubles the previous term and subtracts 1. If it comes up tails, he takes half of the previous term and subtracts 1. What is the probability that the fourth term in Jacob's sequence is an integer?

(A) $\dfrac{1}{6}$

(B) $\dfrac{1}{3}$

(C) $\dfrac{1}{2}$

(D) $\dfrac{5}{8}$

(E) $\dfrac{3}{4}$

26. A poll shows that 70% of all voters approve of the mayor's work. On three separate occasions a pollster selects a voter at random. What is the probability that on exactly one of these three occasions the voter approves of the mayor's work?

(A) 0.063
(B) 0.189
(C) 0.233
(D) 0.333
(E) 0.441

27. A coin is biased in such a way that on each toss the probability of heads is $\frac{2}{3}$ and the probability of tails is $\frac{1}{3}$. The outcomes of the tosses are independent. A player has the choice of playing Game A or Game B. In Game A she tosses the coin three times and wins if all three outcomes are the same. In Game B she tosses the coin four times and wins if both the outcomes of the first and second tosses are the same and the outcomes of the third and fourth tosses are the same. How do the chances of winning Game A compare to the chances of winning Game B?

(A) The probability of winning Game A is $\frac{4}{81}$ less than the probability of winning Game B.

(B) The probability of winning Game A is $\frac{2}{81}$ less than the probability of winning Game B.

(C) The probabilities are the same.

(D) The probability of winning Game A is $\frac{2}{81}$ greater than the probability of winning Game B.

(E) The probability of winning Game A is $\frac{4}{81}$ greater than the probability of winning Game B.

28. Tome, Dick and Harry are playing a game. Starting at the same time, each of them flips a fair coin repeatedly until he gets his first head, at which point he stops. What is the probability that all three flip their coins the same number of times?

(A) $\dfrac{1}{8}$

(B) $\dfrac{1}{7}$

(C) $\dfrac{1}{6}$

(D) $\dfrac{1}{4}$

(E) $\dfrac{1}{3}$

29. An unfair coin lands on heads with a probability of $\dfrac{1}{4}$. When tossed $n > 1$ times, the probability of exactly two heads is the same as the probability of exactly three heads. What is the value of n?

(A) 5

(B) 8

(C) 10

(D) 11

(E) 13

30. At Rachelle's school an A counts 4 points, a B 3 points, a C 2 points, and a D 1 point. Her GPA on the four classes she is taking is computed as the total sum of points divided by 4. She is certain that she will get As in both Mathematics and Science, and at least a C in each of English and History. She thinks she has a $\frac{1}{6}$ chance of getting an A in English, and a $\frac{1}{4}$ chance of getting a B. In History, she has a $\frac{1}{4}$ chance of getting an A, and a $\frac{1}{3}$ chance of getting a B, independently of what she gets in English. What is the probability that Rachelle will get a GPA of at least 3.5?

(A) $\frac{11}{72}$

(B) $\frac{1}{6}$

(C) $\frac{3}{16}$

(D) $\frac{11}{24}$

(E) $\frac{1}{2}$

Chapter 9

➢Plane Geometry 1

Plane Geometry를 공부하기에 앞서서...

Plane Geometry 문제는 피타고라스 정리 또는 닮음(Similar) 또는 Angle을 이용
(Trigonometry) 하던지 특수정리(Menelaus Theorem)등을 이용하여 Equation을 만들어
서 해결해야 한다. 즉, Plane Geometry도 알고 보면 Equation이다!

다음을 보자.

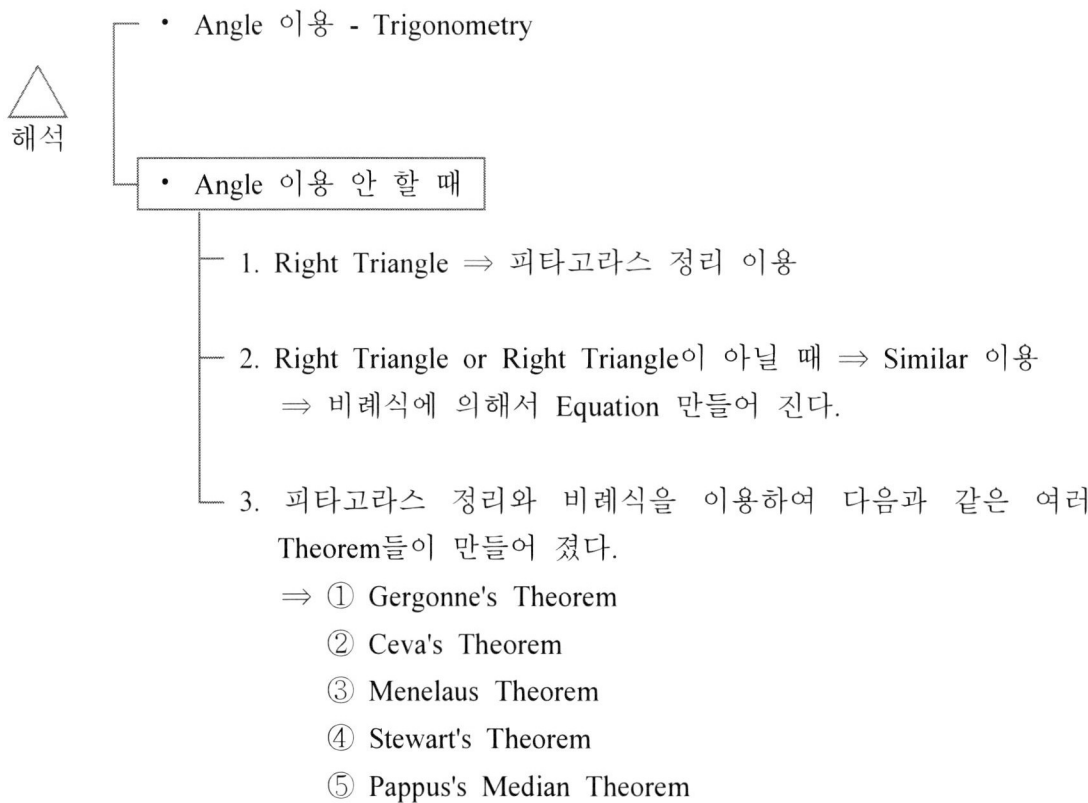

- Angle 이용 - Trigonometry

해석

- Angle 이용 안 할 때

　1. Right Triangle ⇒ 피타고라스 정리 이용

　2. Right Triangle or Right Triangle이 아닐 때 ⇒ Similar 이용
　　⇒ 비례식에 의해서 Equation 만들어 진다.

　3. 피타고라스 정리와 비례식을 이용하여 다음과 같은 여러
　　Theorem들이 만들어 졌다.
　　⇒ ① Gergonne's Theorem
　　　② Ceva's Theorem
　　　③ Menelaus Theorem
　　　④ Stewart's Theorem
　　　⑤ Pappus's Median Theorem
　　　⑥ Ptolemy's Theorem
　　　⑦ Power Theorem
　　　⑧ 각의 이등분 정리(Angle Bisector Theorem)

시작에 앞서서...

Plane Geometry를 공부 할 때, 많은 학생들은 수많은 "정리"들을 암기하고 증명한 후 많은 문제들을 풀어보려고만 한다.

가장 중요한 점은 접근 방법이 정확해야 된다는 것이다. 필자 나름대로의 방법으로 정리 하였다. 필자가 설명하는 내용들을 구구단 암기하듯이 머릿속에 자리 잡고 있어야 한다.

본론으로 들어가보면...

❶ 삼각형(Triangle)은 모든 도형의 세포(Cell)와 같다. 즉, 거의 모든 도형은 삼각형(Triangle)
   으로 구성되어 있다.

❷ 다각형(Polygon)은 모두 삼각형(Triangle)으로 분리된다.

❸ 원(Circle)의 성질도 모두 삼각형(Triangle)에서 나온다.

그러므로, 삼각형만 해결이 된다면 이 세상 도형의 99%는 해결이 되는 것이다.

삼각형을 해석하는 방법을 다음과 같이 분류시키고자 한다. 필자가 제시하는 다음의 분류표를 머릿속에 완전히 주입시키기를 바란다.

 해 석

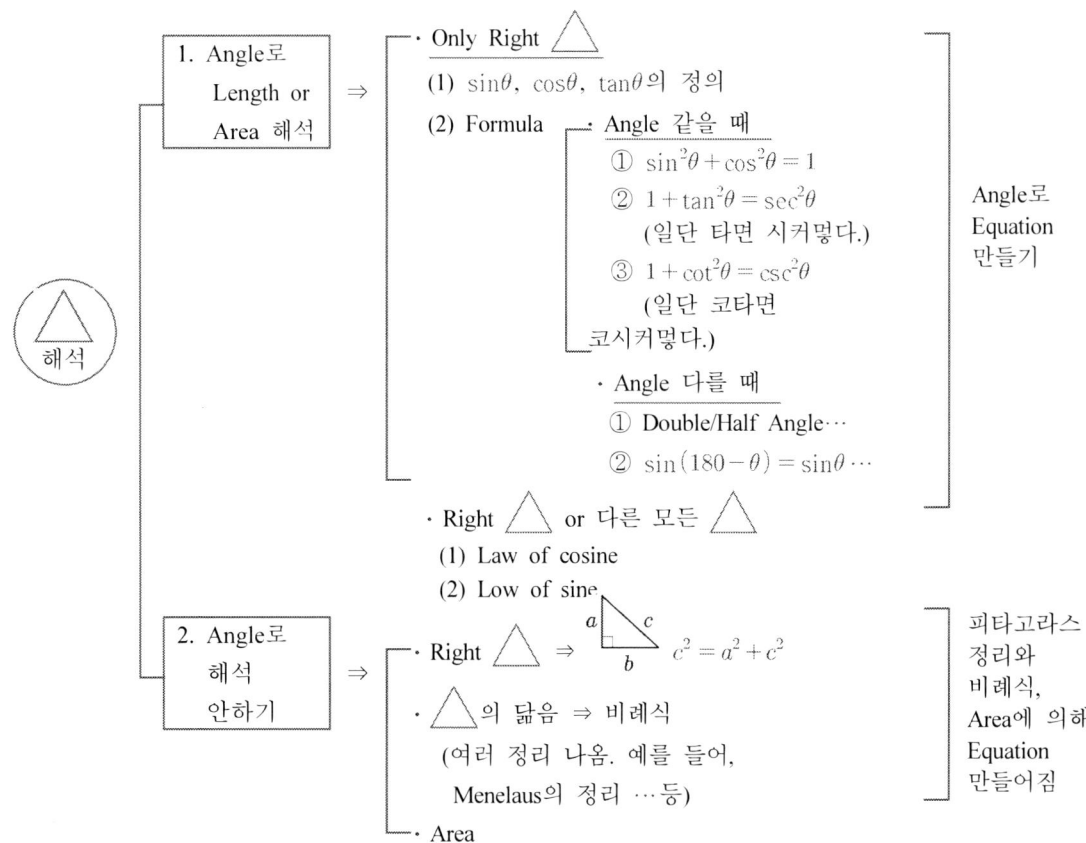

△을 해석한다는 것은 Equation을 푸는 것과 같다. △의 닮음을 찾았다면 바로 비례식이 만들어지고 비례식에 의해서 Equation이 만들어진다. 대부분의 원(Circle)의 성질과 여러 정리들은 거의 95% 이상이 △의 닮음에 의해 나오는 것이다.

우리가 Algebra 2 또는 Precalculus에서 배우는 Trigonometric Function 또한 △을 해석하기 위해서 배우는 것이다. $\sin\theta, \cos\theta, \tan\theta$는 모두 θ와 길이 비로 표현이 되는 것들이다.

"$\sin2\theta = 2\sin\theta\cdot\cos\theta$" 공식을 보면 2θ를 θ로 만드는 과정에서 Equation이 만들어 진다는 것을 알 수 있다. 즉, Angle을 가지고도 △에 대해서 Equation을 만들 수 있다.

결론적으로, Geometry에서 배운 △의 닮음이나 Precalculus 또는 Algebra 2에서 배운 Trigonometric Function 모두 △에서 Equation을 만들어 내기 위해서 배운 것이다.

Circumcenter Theorem

If P is the circumcenter of $\triangle ABC$, then $PB = PA = PC$.

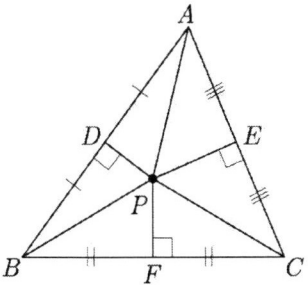

Angle Bisectors

Angle Bisector Theorem

If $\overrightarrow{BF}$ bisects $\angle DBE$, $\overline{FD} \perp \overrightarrow{BD}$, and $\overline{FE} \perp \overrightarrow{BE}$, then $DF = FE$.

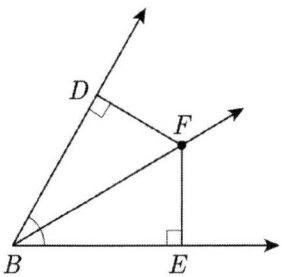

Converse of the Angle Bisector Theorem

If $\overline{FD} \perp \overrightarrow{BD}$, $\overline{FE} \perp \overrightarrow{BE}$, and $DF = FE$, then $\overrightarrow{BF}$ bisects $\angle DBE$.

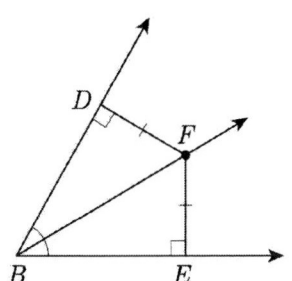

Incenter Theorem

If P is the incenter of $\triangle ABC$, then $PD = PE = PF$

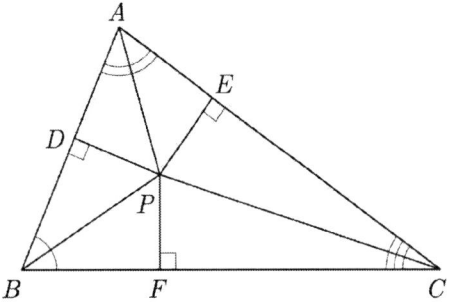

Centroid Theorem

If P is the centroid of $\triangle ABC$, then $AP = \dfrac{2}{3}AK$, $BP = \dfrac{2}{3}BL$, and $CP = \dfrac{2}{3}CJ$.

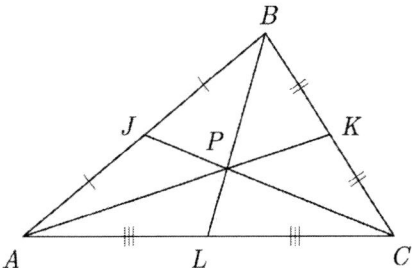

Orthocenter

The lines containing altitudes $\overline{AF}$, $\overline{CD}$, and $\overline{BG}$ intersect at P, the orthocenter of $\triangle ABC$.

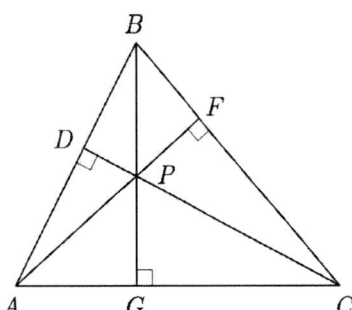

Trapezoid Midsegment Theorem

If $\overline{BE}$ is the midsegment of trapezoid $ACDF$, then $\overline{AF} \parallel \overline{BE}$, $\overline{CD} \parallel \overline{BE}$, and

$$BE = \frac{1}{2}(AF + CD).$$

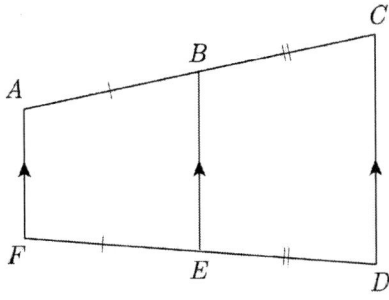

Arcs and Chords

$\overline{FG} \cong \overline{HJ}$ if and only if $\overset{\frown}{FG} \cong \overset{\frown}{HJ}$.

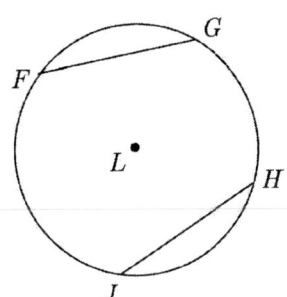

If $\overline{AB}$ is a perpendicular bisector of chord $\overline{XY}$, then $\overline{AB}$ is a diameter of $\odot C$.

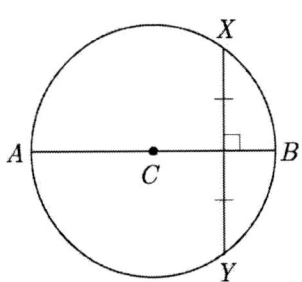

Inscribed Angles
Inscribed Angle Theorem

$$m\angle 1 = \frac{1}{2}m\widehat{AB} \text{ and } m\widehat{AB} = 2m\angle 1$$

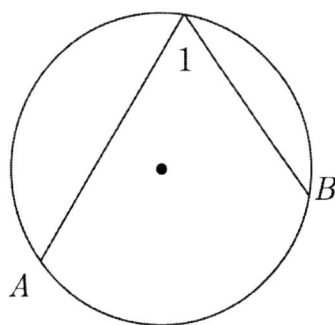

If two inscribed angles of a circle intercept the same arc or congruent arcs, then the angles are congruent.

$\angle B$ and $\angle C$ both intercept $\widehat{AD}$. So, $\angle B \cong \angle C$.

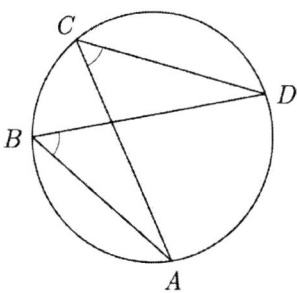

If quadrilateral $KLMN$ is inscribed in $\odot A$, then $\angle L$ and $\angle N$ are supplementary and $\angle K$ and $\angle M$ are supplementary.

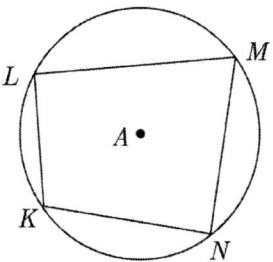

If two segments from the same exterior point are tangent to a circle, then they are congruent.

If $\overline{AB}$ and $\overline{CB}$ are tangent to $\odot D$, then $\overline{AB} \cong \overline{CB}$.

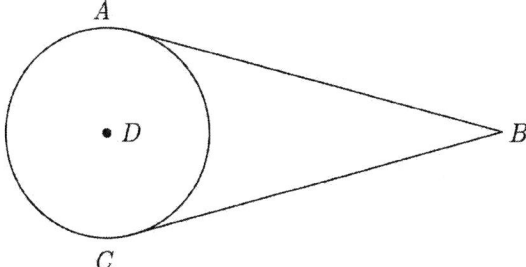

If tangent and a secant intersect in the exterior of a circle, then the square of the measure of the tangent is equal to the product of the measures of the secant and its external secant segment.

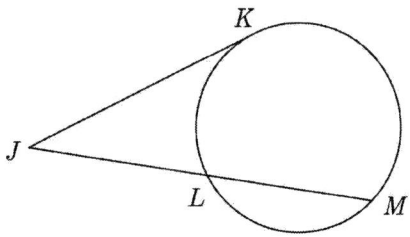

01. The two circles pictured have the same center C. Chord $\overline{AD}$ is tangent to the inner circle at B, AC is 10, and chord $\overline{AD}$ has length 16. What is the area between the two circles?

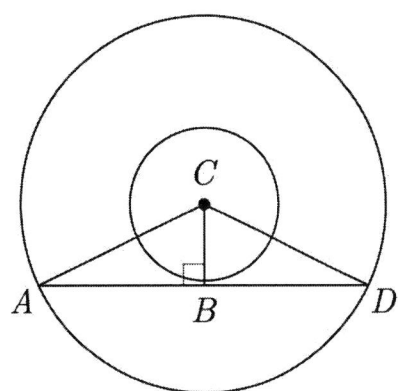

(A) 36π

(B) 49π

(C) 64π

(D) 81π

(E) 100π

02. Semicircles *POQ* and *ROS* pass through the center *O*. What is the ratio of the combined areas of the two semicircles to the area of circle *O*?

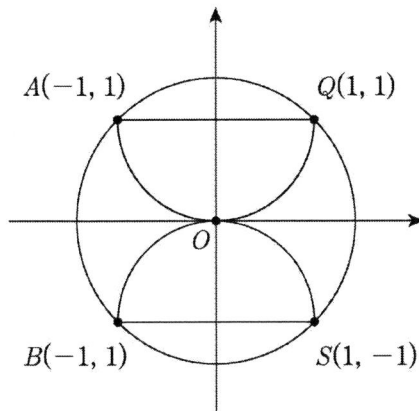

(A) $\dfrac{\sqrt{2}}{4}$

(B) $\dfrac{1}{2}$

(C) $\dfrac{2}{\pi}$

(D) $\dfrac{2}{3}$

(E) $\dfrac{\sqrt{2}}{2}$

03. Quadrilateral $ABCD$ is a trapezoid, $AD=15$, $AB=50$, $BC=20$ and the altitude is 12. What is the area of the trapezoid?

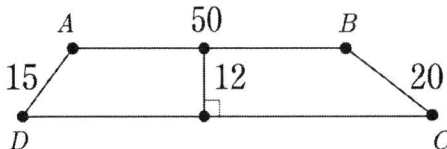

(A) 600

(B) 650

(C) 700

(D) 750

(E) 800

04. A square with area 4 is inscribed in a square with area 5, with one vertex of the smaller square on each side of the larger square. A vertex of the smaller square divides a side of the larger square into two segments, one of length a, and the other of length b. What is the value of ab?

(A) $\dfrac{1}{5}$

(B) $\dfrac{2}{5}$

(C) $\dfrac{1}{2}$

(D) 1

(E) 4

05. Let $ABCD$ be a parallelogram with $\angle ABC = 120°$, $AB = 6$ and $BC = 10$. Extend $\overline{CD}$ through D to E so that $DE = 4$. If $\overline{BE}$ intersects $\overline{AD}$ at F, then $\overline{FD}$ is closest to

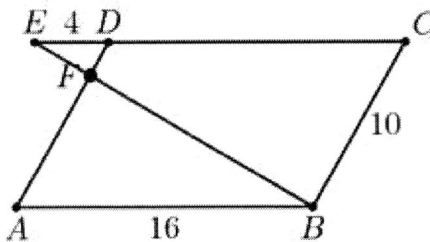

    (A) 1

    (B) 2

    (C) 3

    (D) 4

    (E) 5

06. Circles with centers A and B have radii 3 and 8, respectively. A common internal tangent intersects the circles at C and D, respectively. Lines AB and CD intersect at E, and $AE = 5$. What is CD?

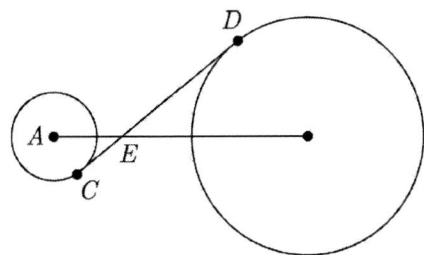

    (A) 13

    (B) $\dfrac{44}{3}$

    (C) $\sqrt{221}$

    (D) $\sqrt{255}$

    (E) $\dfrac{55}{3}$

07. Circles with centers O and P have radii 2 and 4, respectively, and are externally tangent. Points A and B are on the circle centered at O, and points C and D are on the circle centered at P, such that $\overline{AD}$ and $\overline{BC}$ are common external tangents to the circles. What is the area of hexagon $AOBCPD$?

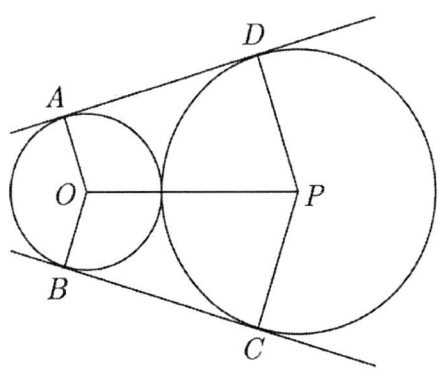

(A) $18\sqrt{3}$

(B) $24\sqrt{2}$

(C) 36

(D) $24\sqrt{3}$

(E) $32\sqrt{2}$

08. Many Gothic cathedrals have windows with portions containing a ring of congruent circles that are circumscribed by a larger circle, In the figure shown, the number of smaller circles is four. What is the ratio of the sum of the areas of the four smaller circles to the area of the larger circle?

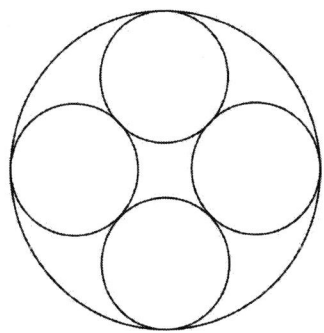

(A) $3 - 2\sqrt{2}$

(B) $2 - \sqrt{2}$

(C) $4(3 - 2\sqrt{2})$

(D) $\dfrac{1}{2}(3 - \sqrt{2})$

(E) $2\sqrt{2} - 2$

09. A circle of radius 1 is surrounded by 4 circles of radius r as shown. What is r?

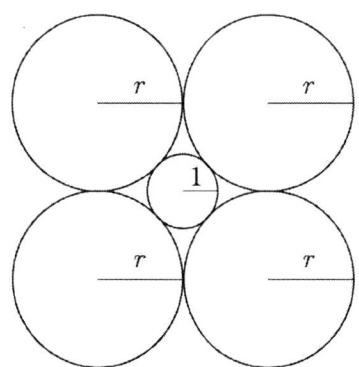

(A) $\sqrt{2}$

(B) $1 + \sqrt{2}$

(C) $\sqrt{6}$

(D) 3

(E) $2 + \sqrt{2}$

10. Right $\triangle ABC$ has $AB = 3$, $BC = 4$, and $AC = 5$. Square $XYZW$ is inscribed in $\triangle ABC$ with X and Y on $\overline{AC}$, W on $\overline{AB}$, and Z on $\overline{BC}$ What is the side length of the square?

(A) $\dfrac{3}{2}$

(B) $\dfrac{60}{37}$

(C) $\dfrac{12}{7}$

(D) $\dfrac{23}{13}$

(E) 2

11. Four circles of radius 1 are each tangent to two sides of a square and externally tangent to a circle of radius 2, as shown. What is the area of the square?

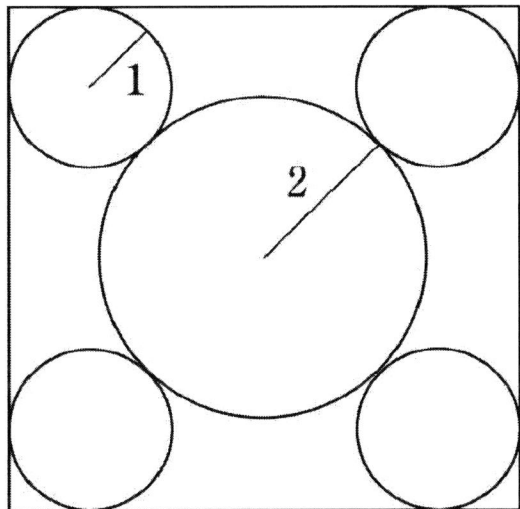

(A) 32

(B) $22 + 12\sqrt{2}$

(C) $16 + 16\sqrt{3}$

(D) 48

(E) $36 + 16\sqrt{2}$

12. Three circles of radius s are drawn in the first quadrant of the xy-plane. The first circle is tangent to both axes, the second is tangent to the first circle and the x-axis, and the third is tangent to the first circle and the y-axis. A circle of radius $r > s$ is tangent to both axes and to the second and third circles. What is r/s?

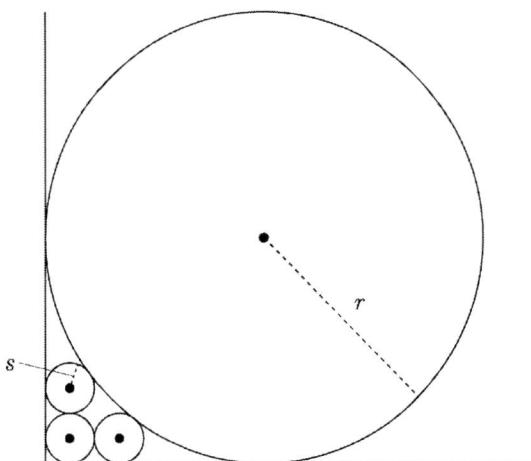

(A) 5

(B) 6

(C) 8

(D) 9

(E) 10

13. A circle of radius 1 is tangent to a circle of radius 2. The sides of $\triangle ABC$ are tangent to the circles as shown, and the sides $\overline{AB}$ and $\overline{AC}$ are congruent. What is the area of $\triangle ABC$?

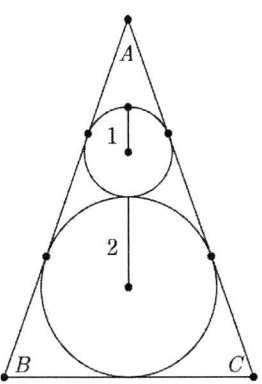

(A) $\dfrac{35}{2}$

(B) $15\sqrt{2}$

(C) $\dfrac{64}{3}$

(D) $16\sqrt{2}$

(E) 24

14. Circles with centers P, Q and R, having radii 1, 2 and 3, respectively, lie on the same side of line l and are tangent to l at P', Q' and R', respectively, with Q' between P' and R'. The circle with center Q is externally tangent to each of the other two circles. What is the area of triangle PQR?

(A) 0

(B) $\sqrt{\dfrac{2}{3}}$

(C) 1

(D) $\sqrt{6} - \sqrt{2}$

(E) $\sqrt{\dfrac{3}{2}}$

15. The figure below shows two parallel lines, ℓ and m, that are distance 12 apart :

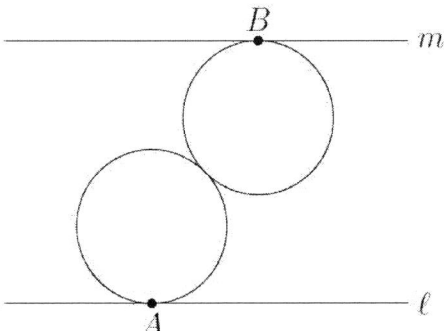

A circle is tangent to line ℓ at point A. Another circle is tangent to line m at point B. The two circles are congruent and tangent to each other as shown. The distance between A and B is 13. What is the radius of each circle?

(A) $\dfrac{169}{48}$

(B) $\dfrac{13}{48}$

(C) $\dfrac{1}{2}$

(D) $\dfrac{49}{12}$

(E) 4

16. Square $ABCD$ has side length 2. A semicircle with diameter $\overline{AB}$ is constructed inside the square, and the tangent to the semicircle from C intersects side $\overline{AD}$ at E. What is the length of $\overline{CE}$?

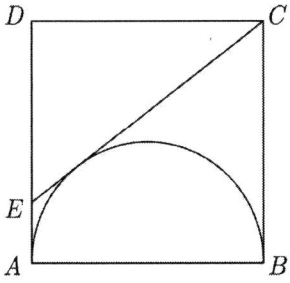

(A) $\dfrac{2+\sqrt{5}}{2}$

(B) $\sqrt{5}$

(C) $\sqrt{6}$

(D) $\dfrac{5}{2}$

(E) $5-\sqrt{5}$

17. Circles A, B, and C are externally tangent to each other and internally tangent to circle D. Circles B and C are congruent. Circle A has radius 1 and passes through the center of D. What is the radius of circle B?

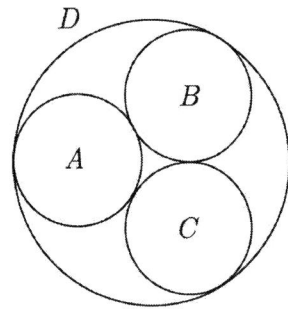

(A) $\dfrac{2}{3}$

(B) $\dfrac{\sqrt{3}}{2}$

(C) $\dfrac{7}{8}$

(D) $\dfrac{8}{9}$

(E) $\dfrac{1+\sqrt{3}}{3}$

18. In rectangle $ABCD$, we have $AB=8$, $BC=9$, H is on BC with $BH=6$, E is on AD with $DE=4$, line EC intersects line AH at G, and F is on line AD with $GF\perp AF$. Find the length of GF.

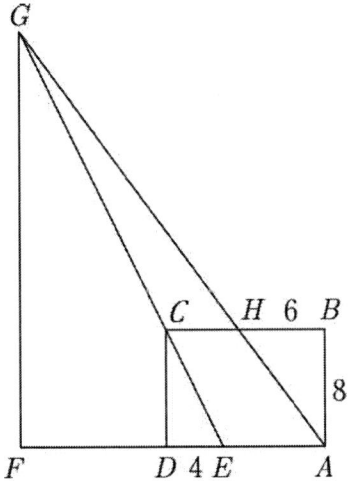

(A) 16

(B) 20

(C) 24

(D) 28

(E) 30

19. In trapezoid $ABCD$ with bases AB and CD, we have $AB=52$, $BC=12$, $CD=39$, and $DA=5$ (diagram not to scale). The area of $ABCD$ is

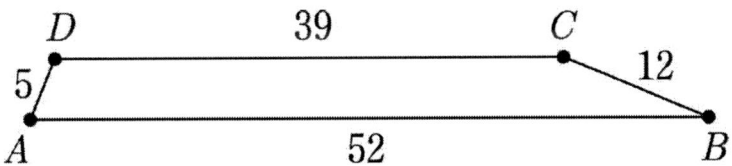

(A) 182

(B) 195

(C) 210

(D) 234

(E) 260

20. Triangle PQR has side-lengths $PQ=12$, $QR=24$, and $PR=18$. The line through the incenter of $\triangle PQR$ parallel to $\overline{QR}$ intersects $\overline{PQ}$ at S and $\overline{PR}$ at T. What is the perimeter of $\triangle PST$?

(A) 27

(B) 30

(C) 33

(D) 36

(E) 42

21. Spot's doghouse has a regular hexagonal base that measures one yard on each side. He is tethered to a vertex with a two-yard rope. What is the area, in square yards, of the region outside of the doghouse that Spot can reach?

(A) $\dfrac{2\pi}{3}$

(B) 2π

(C) $\dfrac{5\pi}{2}$

(D) $\dfrac{8\pi}{3}$

(E) 3π

22. Externally tangent circles with centers at points A and B have radii of lengths 5 and 3, respectively. A line externally tangent to both circles intersects ray AB at point C. What is BC?

(A) 4

(B) 4.8

(C) 10.2

(D) 12

(E) 14.4

23. A semicircle of diameter 1 sits at the top of a semicircle of diameter 2, as shown. The shaded area inside the smaller semicircle and outside the larger semicircle is called a lune. Determine the area of this lune.

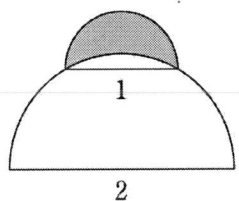

(A) $\dfrac{1}{6}\pi - \dfrac{\sqrt{3}}{4}$

(B) $\dfrac{\sqrt{3}}{4} - \dfrac{1}{12}\pi$

(C) $\dfrac{\sqrt{3}}{4} - \dfrac{1}{24}\pi$

(D) $\dfrac{\sqrt{3}}{4} + \dfrac{1}{24}\pi$

(E) $\dfrac{\sqrt{3}}{4} + \dfrac{1}{12}\pi$

24. Circles centered at A and B each have radius 2, as shown. Point O is the midpoint of $\overline{AB}$, and $OA = 2\sqrt{2}$. Segments OC and OD are tangent to the circles centered at A and B, respectively, and EF is a common tangent. What is the area of the shaded region $ECODF$?

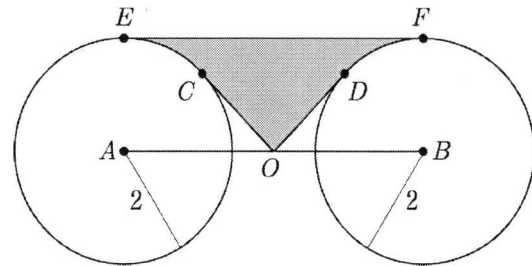

(A) $\dfrac{8\sqrt{2}}{3}$

(B) $8\sqrt{2} - 4 - \pi$

(C) $4\sqrt{2}$

(D) $4\sqrt{2} + \dfrac{\pi}{8}$

(E) $8\sqrt{2} - 2 - \dfrac{\pi}{2}$

25. A triangle is partitioned into three triangles and a quadrilateral by drawing two lines from vertices to their opposite sides. The areas of the three triangles are 3, 7, and 7, as shown. What is the area of the shaded quadrilateral?

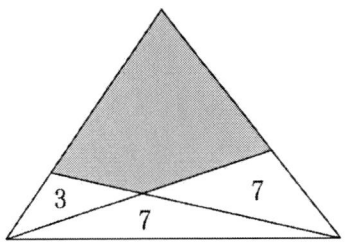

(A) 15

(B) 17

(C) $\dfrac{35}{2}$

(D) 18

(E) $\dfrac{55}{3}$

26. Trapezoid $ABCD$ has bases $\overline{AB}$ and $\overline{CD}$ and diagonals intersecting at K. Suppose that $AB=9$, $DC=12$, and the area of $\triangle AKD$ is 24. What is the area of trapezoid $ABCD$?

(A) 92

(B) 94

(C) 96

(D) 98

(E) 100

27. A point P is selected at random from the interior of the pentagon with vertices $A=(0, 2)$, $B=(4, 0)$, $C=(2\pi+1, 0)$, $D=(2\pi+1, 4)$, and $E=(0, 4)$. What is the probability that $\angle APB$ is obtuse?

(A) $\dfrac{1}{5}$

(B) $\dfrac{1}{4}$

(C) $\dfrac{5}{16}$

(D) $\dfrac{3}{8}$

(E) $\dfrac{1}{2}$

28. Square $ABCD$ has side length s, a circle centered at E has radius r, and r and s are both rational. The circle passes through D, and D lies on $\overline{BE}$. Point F lies on the circle, on the same side of $\overline{BE}$ as A. Segment AF is tangent to the circle, and $AF=\sqrt{9+5\sqrt{2}}$. What is r/s?

(A) $\dfrac{1}{2}$

(B) $\dfrac{5}{9}$

(C) $\dfrac{3}{5}$

(D) $\dfrac{5}{3}$

(E) $\dfrac{9}{5}$

158

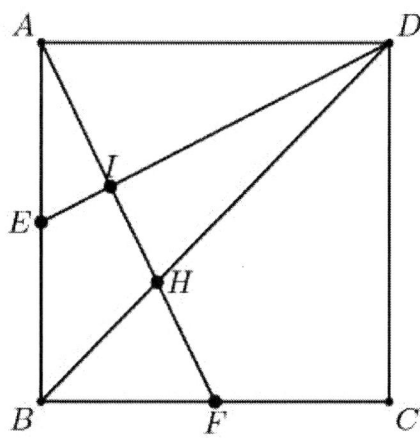

29. If $ABCD$ is a 2×2 square, E is the midpoint of $\overline{AB}$, F is the midpoint of $\overline{BC}$, $\overline{AF}$ and $\overline{DE}$ intersect at I, and $\overline{BD}$ and $\overline{AF}$ intersect at H, then the area of quadrilateral $BEIH$ is

(A) $\dfrac{1}{3}$

(B) $\dfrac{2}{5}$

(C) $\dfrac{7}{15}$

(D) $\dfrac{8}{15}$

(E) $\dfrac{3}{5}$

30. Rectangle $ABCD$ has $AB=5$ and $BC=4$. Point E lies on $\overline{AB}$ so that $EB=1$, point G lies on $\overline{BC}$ so that $CG=1$, and point F lies on $\overline{CD}$ so that $DF=2$. Segments $\overline{AG}$ and $\overline{AC}$ intersect $\overline{EF}$ at Q and P, respectively. What is the value of $\dfrac{PQ}{EF}$?

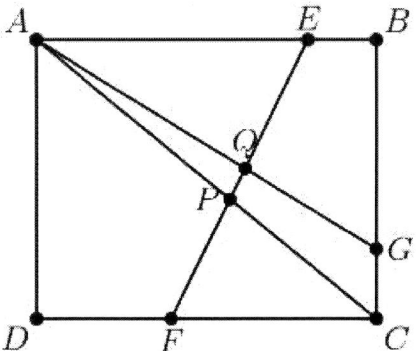

(A) $\dfrac{\sqrt{13}}{16}$

(B) $\dfrac{\sqrt{2}}{13}$

(C) $\dfrac{9}{82}$

(D) $\dfrac{10}{91}$

(E) $\dfrac{1}{9}$

31. In rectangle $ABCD$, $AB=6$ and $BC=3$. Point E between B and C, and point F between E and C are such that $BE=EF=FC$. Segments $\overline{AE}$ and $\overline{AF}$ intersect $\overline{BD}$ at P and Q, respectively. The ratio $BP:PQ:QD$ can be written as $r:s:t$ where the greatest common factor of r, s and t is 1. What is $r+s+t$?

(A) 7

(B) 9

(C) 12

(D) 15

(E) 20

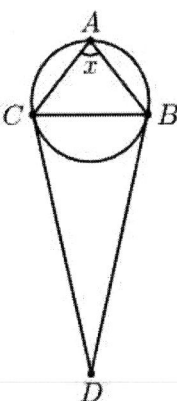

32. In acute isosceles triangle, ABC, is inscribed in a circle. Through B and C, tangents to the circle are drawn, meeting at point D. If $\angle ABC = \angle ACB = 2\angle D$ and x is the radian measure of $\angle A$, then $x =$

(A) $\dfrac{3\pi}{7}$

(B) $\dfrac{4\pi}{9}$

(C) $\dfrac{5\pi}{11}$

(D) $\dfrac{6\pi}{13}$

(E) $\dfrac{7\pi}{15}$

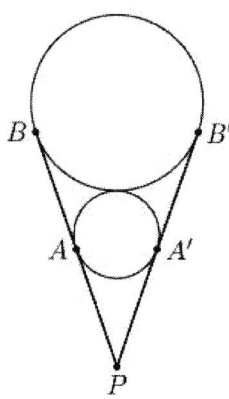

33. Two circles are externally tangent. Lines $\overline{PAB}$ and $\overline{PA'B'}$ are common tangents with A and A' on the smaller circle B and B' on the larger circle. If $PA = AB = 4$, then the area of the smaller circle is

(A) 1.44π

(B) 2π

(C) 2.56π

(D) $\sqrt{8}\,\pi$

(E) 4π

34. A square of perimeter 20 is inscribed in a square of perimeter 28. What is the greatest distance between a vertex of the inner square and a vertex of the outer square?

(A) $\sqrt{58}$

(B) $\dfrac{7\sqrt{5}}{2}$

(C) 8

(D) $\sqrt{65}$

(E) $5\sqrt{3}$

35. A square region $ABCD$ is externally tangent to the circle with equation $x^2 + y^2 = 1$ at the point $(0,1)$ on the side CD. Vertices A and B are on the circle with equation $x^2 + y^2 = 4$. What is the side length of this square?

(A) $\dfrac{\sqrt{10}+5}{10}$

(B) $\dfrac{2\sqrt{5}}{5}$

(C) $\dfrac{2\sqrt{2}}{3}$

(D) $\dfrac{2\sqrt{19}-4}{5}$

(E) $\dfrac{9-\sqrt{17}}{5}$

36. Triangle ABC has $AB = 27$, $AC = 26$ and $BC = 25$. Let I denote the intersection of the internal angle bisectors of $\triangle ABC$. What is BI?

(A) 15

(B) $5 + \sqrt{26} + 3\sqrt{3}$

(C) $3\sqrt{26}$

(D) $\dfrac{2}{3}\sqrt{546}$

(E) $9\sqrt{3}$

37. Point P is inside equilateral $\triangle ABC$. Points Q, R, and S are the feet of the perpendiculars from P to $\overline{AB}$, $\overline{BC}$, and $\overline{CA}$, respectively. Given that $PQ=1$, $PR=2$, and $PS=3$, what is AB?

(A) 4

(B) $3\sqrt{3}$

(C) 6

(D) $4\sqrt{3}$

(E) 9

38. Two parallel chords in a circle have lengths 10 and 14, and the distance between them is 6. The chord parallel to these chords and midway between them is of length $\sqrt{a}$ where a is

(A) 144

(B) 156

(C) 168

(D) 176

(E) 184

164

39. Let $ABCD$ be an isosceles trapezoid such that $AD = BC$, $AB = 3$, and $CD = 8$. Let E be a point in the plane such that $BC = EC$ and $AE \perp EC$. What is AE ?

(A) $2\sqrt{6}$

(B) 5

(C) 6

(D) $\sqrt{26}$

(E) $3\sqrt{3}$

40. Let $ABCD$ be a quadrilateral with $\angle BAD = \angle ABC = 90°$, and suppose $AB = BC = 1$, $AD = 2$. The circumcircle of ABC meets $\overline{AD}$ and $\overline{BD}$ at points E and F, respectively. If lines AF and CD meet at K, what is EK ?

(A) $\dfrac{\sqrt{2}}{2}$

(B) $\dfrac{\sqrt{2}}{3}$

(C) $\dfrac{\sqrt{2}}{4}$

(D) $\dfrac{\sqrt{2}}{5}$

(E) $\dfrac{\sqrt{2}}{6}$

41. Let *ABCD* be a square of side length 13. Let *E* and *F* be points on rays *AB* and *AD*, respectively, so that the area of square *ABCD* equals the area of triangle *AEF*. If *EF* intersects *BC* at *X* and *BX* = 6, what is *DF* ?

(A) $2\sqrt{3}$

(B) $\sqrt{13}$

(C) $\sqrt{15}$

(D) 4

(E) 5

Chapter 10

➢Plane Geometry 2

1. Angle로 Length or Area 해석

(1) $\sin\theta, \cos\theta, \tan\theta$는 Right △에서 정의가 된다.

    : 간단하지만 상당히 중요한 내용이다. 즉, $\sin\theta, \cos\theta, \tan\theta$의 정의를 쓰고 싶다면 보조선을   그어서라도 Right △을 만들어야 한다.

(2) Formula

    : 무조건 암기해야 한다.

    ①   Angle 같을 때 $\Rightarrow$ · $\sin^2\theta + \cos^2\theta = 1$

                                 · $1 + \tan^2\theta = \sec^2\theta$ (일단 타면 시커멓다.)

                                 · $1 + \cot^2\theta = \csc^2\theta$ (일단 코타면 코시커멓다.)

    ② Angle 다를 때 $\Rightarrow$ 2θ를 θ로 만들고 3θ를 θ로 만드는 과정에서 Equation이 만들어 진다. 주어진 문제에서 특별한 조건이 없더라도 Angle만 가지고도

                  Equation을 이끌어 내야 한다.

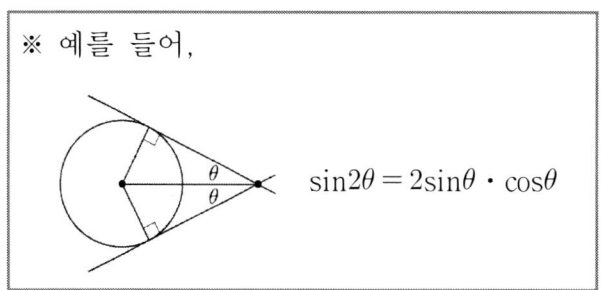

※ 예를 들어,

$$\sin 2\theta = 2\sin\theta \cdot \cos\theta$$

다음의 공식들은 모두 암기하여야 한다.

다른 Angle로 Equation 만드는 Formulas

Sum and Difference

- $\sin(\alpha \pm \beta) = \sin\alpha\cos\beta \pm \cos\alpha\sin\beta$
- $\cos(\alpha \pm \beta) = \cos\alpha\cos\beta \mp \sin\alpha\sin\beta$
- $\tan(\alpha \pm \beta) = \dfrac{\tan\alpha \pm \tan\beta}{1 \mp \tan\alpha \cdot \tan\beta}$

Double Angle

- $\sin2\alpha = 2\sin\alpha\cos\alpha$
- $\cos2\alpha = \cos^2\alpha - \sin^2\alpha$

$\qquad = 1 - 2\sin^2\alpha$

$\qquad = 2\cos^2\alpha - 1$

- $\tan2\alpha = \dfrac{2\tan\alpha}{1-\tan^2\alpha}$

Power − Reduce

- $\sin^2\dfrac{\alpha}{2} = \dfrac{1-\cos\alpha}{2}$
- $\cos^2\dfrac{\alpha}{2} = \dfrac{1+\cos\alpha}{2}$
- $\tan^2\dfrac{\alpha}{2} = \dfrac{1-\cos\alpha}{1+\cos\alpha}$

Triple Angle

- $\sin3\alpha = 3\sin\alpha - 4\sin^3\alpha$
- $\cos3\alpha = 4\cos^3\alpha - 3\cos\alpha$

Sum/Difference ⇔ Product

- $\sin\alpha + \sin\beta = 2\sin\dfrac{\alpha+\beta}{2} \cdot \cos\dfrac{\alpha-\beta}{2}$
- $\sin\alpha - \sin\beta = 2\cos\dfrac{\alpha+\beta}{2} \cdot \sin\dfrac{\alpha-\beta}{2}$
- $\cos\alpha + \cos\beta = 2\cos\dfrac{\alpha+\beta}{2} \cdot \cos\dfrac{\alpha-\beta}{2}$
- $\cos\alpha - \cos\beta = -2\sin\dfrac{\alpha+\beta}{2} \cdot \sin\dfrac{\alpha-\beta}{2}$

$\sin\alpha \cdot \sin\beta = -\dfrac{1}{2}\{\cos(\alpha+\beta) - \cos(\alpha-\beta)\}$

Product ⇔ Sum/Difference

- $\sin\alpha \cdot \cos\beta = \dfrac{1}{2}\{\sin(\alpha+\beta) + \sin(\alpha-\beta)\}$
- $\cos\alpha \cdot \sin\beta = \dfrac{1}{2}\{\sin(\alpha+\beta) - \sin(\alpha-\beta)\}$
- $\cos\alpha \cdot \cos\beta = \dfrac{1}{2}\{\cos(\alpha+\beta) + \cos(\alpha-\beta)\}$

$$\sin(\pi - \theta) = \sin\theta, \qquad \sin\left(\frac{3}{2}\pi + \theta\right) = -\cos\theta$$

$$\cos(\pi - \theta) = -\cos\theta \qquad \tan(\pi - \theta) = -\tan\theta$$

$$\sin\left(\frac{\pi}{2} + \theta\right) = \cos\theta \qquad \tan\left(\frac{\pi}{2} + \theta\right) = -\cot\theta$$

$$\cos(2\pi - \theta) = \cos\theta \qquad \sin(\pi + \theta) = -\sin\theta \ \cdots 등등$$

Sine으로 합성하기

· $\sin\alpha + \sin\beta$ ┐ 이 4가지는 Sum/Difference를
· $\sin\alpha - \sin\beta$ │ 모두 Product 공식으로 바꿀 수 있다.
· $\cos\alpha + \cos\beta$ │ sine끼리 $+$ $-$하든가 cosine끼리 $+$ $-$할 때...
· $\cos\alpha - \cos\beta$ ┘ 그리고 Angle α, β로 다를 때에는 공식이 존재!

$\Rightarrow$ But! sine과 cosine을 $\pm$하고 Angle이 같을 때에는 다음과 같이 할 수 있다.

(EX) ① $\sqrt{3}\sin\theta + \cos\theta \Rightarrow \sin\theta$ 앞의 $\sqrt{3}$ 는 무조건 x

$\cos\theta$ 앞의 1은 무조건 y

$\Rightarrow$ ② 그린다.

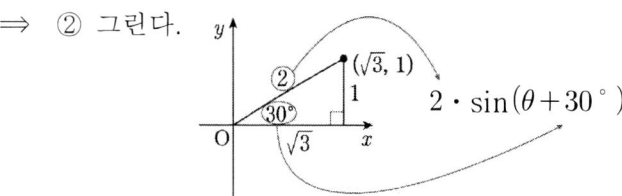

$2 \cdot \sin(\theta + 30°)$

(Proof)

$$2\sin(\theta + 30°) = 2\sin\theta \cdot \cos30° + 2\cos\theta \cdot \sin30° = 2 \cdot \frac{\sqrt{3}}{2} \cdot \sin\theta + 2 \cdot \frac{1}{2}\cos\theta$$

$$= \sqrt{3}\sin\theta + \cos\theta$$

01. From the diagram shown below, what is the length of $\overline{AB}$?

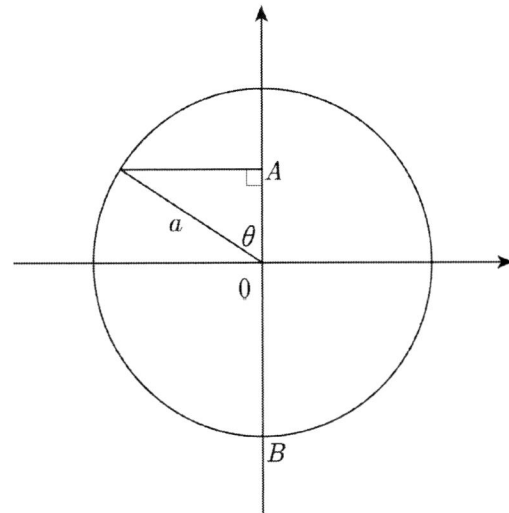

(A) $\sin\theta$

(B) $\tan\theta$

(C) $a - a\sin\theta$

(D) $a + a\cos\theta$

(E) $a + a\sin\theta$

02. Which of the following is equal to $-\sin x$?

(A) $\cos\left(\dfrac{\pi}{2} + x\right)$

(B) $\cos\left(\dfrac{\pi}{2} - x\right)$

(C) $\cos(\pi - x)$

(D) $\cos(\pi + x)$

(E) $\cos(2\pi - x)$

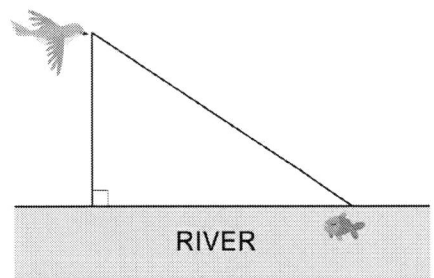

RIVER

03. In the figure above, a bird is flying over the river parallel to the surface. The depression angle of the bird gazing down at the fish in the river is $30°$. When direct distance from bird to fish is $12\,\mathrm{ft}$, how high is the bird flying from the surface of the river?

    (A) $4\,\mathrm{ft}$

    (B) $4\sqrt{3}\,\mathrm{ft}$

    (C) $6\,\mathrm{ft}$

    (D) $6\sqrt{2}\,\mathrm{ft}$

    (E) $6\sqrt{3}\,\mathrm{ft}$

04. For two lines l_1 and l_2, $l_1 : y = \sqrt{3}\,x + 1$ and $l_2 : y = \dfrac{1}{\sqrt{3}}x + 1$. If the angle between two lines l_1 and l_2 is θ, what is the value of $\sin\theta$?

    (A) $\dfrac{1}{2}$

    (B) $\dfrac{\sqrt{2}}{2}$

    (C) $\dfrac{\sqrt{3}}{2}$

    (D) 1

    (E) None of the above

Andy   Julia

05. As the figure, Andy was traveling on the level road at the angle of $75°$ for $20\,\text{m}$. Julia started traveling at the angle of $60°$ in the opposite direction and met Andy. What is the distance between Andy and Julia before they started traveling?

    (A) 6

    (B) $\dfrac{20}{3}$

    (C) $\dfrac{20\sqrt{3}}{3}$

    (D) $\dfrac{20\sqrt{6}}{3}$

    (E) 14

06. In a certain circle, if the chord of a $30-$degree arc is 8 inches long, what is the radius of this circle?

    (A) 6.00

    (B) 8.00

    (C) $8\sqrt{2}$

    (D) $8\sqrt{2+\sqrt{3}}$

    (E) $16\sqrt{2+\sqrt{3}}$

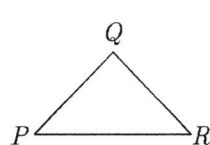 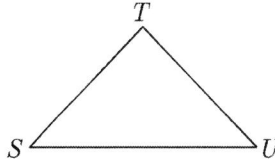

07. The two triangles above $\triangle PQR$ and $\triangle STU$ are similar. When $\overline{PQ}=10$, $\overline{ST}=15$ $\sin R=\dfrac{1}{3}$, and $\sin P=\dfrac{1}{5}$, what is the length of $\overline{TU}$?

(A) 8

(B) 9

(C) 12

(D) 13

(E) 15

08. $\cos(A-B)+\sin(3B)=2$. If the length of $\overline{BC}$ of $\triangle ABC$ is 8, What is the length of $\overline{AB}$?

(A) 8

(B) $8\sqrt{2}$

(C) $8\sqrt{3}$

(D) $12\sqrt{2}$

(E) $12\sqrt{3}$

09. What is the maximum value of $\sqrt{3}\,\sin\theta - \cos\theta$?

(A) 1

(B) 2

(C) 3

(D) 4

(E) 5

10. Find the value of $\dfrac{Mmp}{\pi}$, when the maximum of a function

$y = \sin\theta - \sqrt{3}\,\cos\theta + 3$ is M, the minimum is m, and the period is p.

(A) 6

(B) 8

(C) 10

(D) 12

(E) 14

01. Equilateral $\triangle ABC$ has side length 2, M is the midpoint of $\overline{AC}$, and C is the midpoint of $\overline{BD}$. What is the area of $\triangle CDM$?

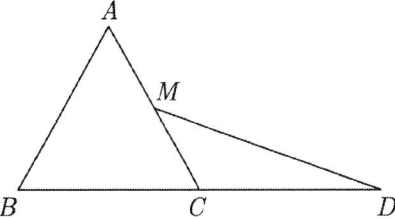

(A) $\dfrac{\sqrt{2}}{2}$

(B) $\dfrac{3}{4}$

(C) $\dfrac{\sqrt{3}}{2}$

(D) 1

(E) $\sqrt{2}$

02. In rectangle $ABCD$, angle C is trisected by $\overline{CF}$ and $\overline{CE}$, where E is on $\overline{AB}$, F is on $\overline{AD}$, $BE=6$ and $AF=2$. Which of the following is closest to the area of the rectangle $ABCD$?

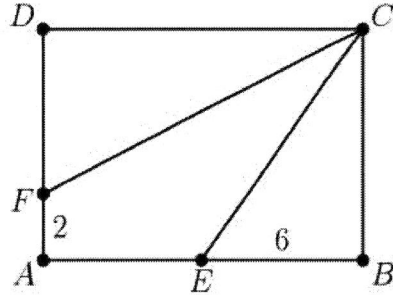

(A) 110

(B) 120

(C) 130

(D) 140

(E) 150

03. Points K, L, M, and N lie in the plane of the square $ABCD$ such that AKB, BLC, CMD, and DNA are equilateral triangles. If $ABCD$ has an area of 16, find the area of $KLMN$.

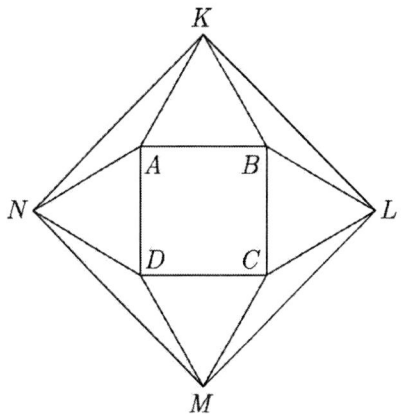

(A) 32

(B) $16 + 16\sqrt{3}$

(C) 48

(D) $32 + 16\sqrt{3}$

(E) 64

04. Rhombus $ABCD$, with a side length 6, is rolled to form a cylinder of volume 6 by taping $\overline{AB}$ to $\overline{DC}$. What is $\sin(\angle ABC)$?

(A) $\dfrac{\pi}{9}$

(B) $\dfrac{1}{2}$

(C) $\dfrac{\pi}{6}$

(D) $\dfrac{\pi}{4}$

(E) $\dfrac{\sqrt{3}}{2}$

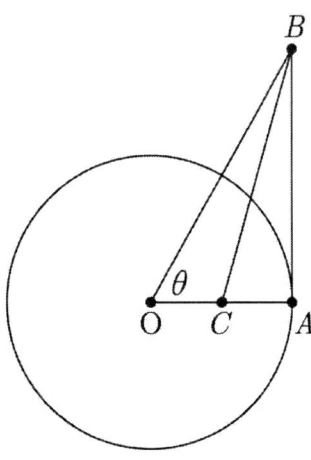

05. A circle centered at O has radius 1 and contains the point A. The segment AB is tangent to the circle at A and $\angle AOB = \theta$. If point C lies on $\overline{OA}$ and $\overline{BC}$ bisects $\angle ABO$, then $OC =$

(A) $\sec^2\theta - \tan\theta$

(B) $\dfrac{1}{2}$

(C) $\dfrac{\cos^2\theta}{1 + \sin\theta}$

(D) $\dfrac{1}{1 + \sin\theta}$

(E) $\dfrac{\sin\theta}{\cos^2\theta}$

06. Square $ABCD$ has sides of length 4, and M is the midpoint of $\overline{CD}$. A circle with radius 2 and center M intersects a circle with radius 4 and center A at points P and D. What is the distance from P to $\overline{AD}$?

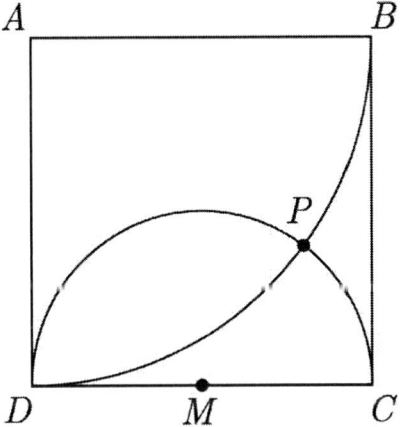

(A) 3

(B) $\dfrac{16}{5}$

(C) $\dfrac{13}{4}$

(D) $2\sqrt{3}$

(E) $\dfrac{7}{2}$

07. The midpoints of the sides of a regular hexagon $ABCDEF$ are joined to form a smaller hexagon. What fraction of the area of $ABCDEF$ is enclosed by the smaller hexagon?

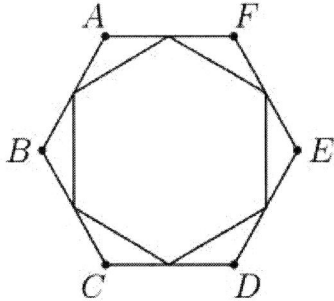

(A) $\dfrac{1}{2}$

(B) $\dfrac{\sqrt{3}}{3}$

(C) $\dfrac{2}{3}$

(D) $\dfrac{3}{4}$

(E) $\dfrac{\sqrt{3}}{2}$

08. Equilateral triangle DEF is inscribed in equilateral triangle ABC such that $\overline{DE} \perp \overline{BC}$. The ratio of the area of $\triangle DEF$ to the area of $\triangle ABC$ is

(A) $\dfrac{1}{6}$

(B) $\dfrac{1}{4}$

(C) $\dfrac{1}{3}$

(D) $\dfrac{2}{5}$

(E) $\dfrac{1}{2}$

09. In $\triangle ABC$, $\angle ABC = 120°$, $AB = 3$ and $BC = 4$. If perpendiculars constructed to $\overline{AB}$ at A and to $\overline{BC}$ at C meet at D, then $CD =$

(A) 3

(B) $\dfrac{8}{\sqrt{3}}$

(C) 5

(D) $\dfrac{11}{2}$

(E) $\dfrac{10}{\sqrt{3}}$

10. Equilateral triangle ABC has P on AB and Q on AC. The triangle is folded along PQ so that vertex A now rests at A' on side BC. If $BA' = 1$ and $A'C = 2$ then the length of the crease PQ is

(A) $\dfrac{8}{5}$

(B) $\dfrac{7}{20}\sqrt{21}$

(C) $\dfrac{1 + \sqrt{5}}{2}$

(D) $\dfrac{13}{8}$

(E) $\sqrt{3}$

11. In $\triangle ABC$, $\angle ABC = 45°$. Point D is on $\overline{BC}$ so that $2 \cdot BD = CD$ and $\angle DAB = 15°$. Find $\angle ACB$.

(A) $54°$

(B) $60°$

(C) $72°$

(D) $75°$

(E) $90°$

12. In $\triangle ABC$, we have $AB = 1$ and $AC = 2$. Side $\overline{BC}$ and the median from A to $\overline{BC}$ have the same length. What is BC?

(A) $\dfrac{1 + \sqrt{2}}{2}$

(B) $\dfrac{1 + \sqrt{3}}{2}$

(C) $\sqrt{2}$

(D) $\dfrac{3}{2}$

(E) $\sqrt{3}$

13. Points E and F are located on square $ABCD$ so that $\triangle BEF$ is equilateral. What is the ratio of the area of $\triangle DEF$ to that of $\triangle ABE$?

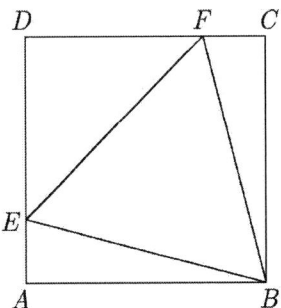

(A) $\dfrac{4}{3}$

(B) $\dfrac{3}{2}$

(C) $\sqrt{3}$

(D) 2

(E) $1+\sqrt{3}$

14. An object moves 8cm in a straight line from A to B, turns at an angle α, measured in radians and chosen at random from the interval $(0,\ \pi)$, and moves 5cm in a straight line to C. What is the probability that $AC < 7$?

(A) $\dfrac{1}{2}$

(B) $\dfrac{1}{3}$

(C) $\dfrac{1}{4}$

(D) $\dfrac{1}{5}$

(E) $\dfrac{1}{6}$

15. In regular hexagon $ABCDEF$, point W, X, Y, and Z are chosen on sides $\overline{BC}$, $\overline{CD}$, $\overline{EF}$, and $\overline{FA}$ respectively, so lines AB, ZW, YX, and ED are parallel and equally spaced. What is the ratio of the area of hexagon $WCXYFZ$ to the area of hexagon $ABCDEF$?

(A) $\dfrac{1}{3}$

(B) $\dfrac{10}{27}$

(C) $\dfrac{11}{27}$

(D) $\dfrac{4}{9}$

(E) $\dfrac{13}{27}$

16. Two rays with common endpoint O forms a $30°$ angle. Point A lies on one ray, point B on the other ray, and $AB=1$. The maximum possible length of OB is

(A) 1

(B) $\dfrac{1+\sqrt{3}}{\sqrt{2}}$

(C) $\sqrt{3}$

(D) 2

(E) $\dfrac{4}{\sqrt{3}}$

17. Points A, B and C on a circle of radius r are situated so that $AB = AC$, $AB > r$, and the length of minor arc BC is r. If angles are measured in radians, then $AB/BC =$

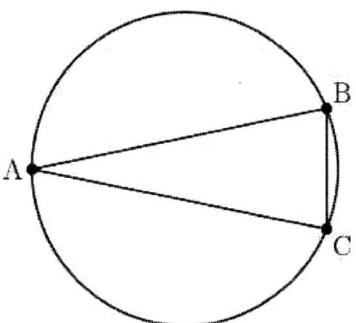

(A) $\dfrac{1}{2} \csc \dfrac{1}{4}$

(B) $2\cos \dfrac{1}{2}$

(C) $4\sin \dfrac{1}{2}$

(D) $\csc \dfrac{1}{2}$

(E) $2\sec \dfrac{1}{2}$

18. A round table has radius 4. Six rectangular place mats are placed on the table. Each place mat has width 1 and length x as shown. They are positioned so that each mat has two corners on the edge of the table, these two corners being end points of the same side of length x. Further, the mats are positioned so that the inner corners each touch an inner corner of an adjacent mat. What is x?

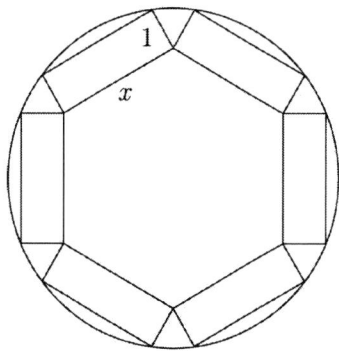

(A) $2\sqrt{5} - \sqrt{3}$

(B) 3

(C) $\dfrac{3\sqrt{7} - \sqrt{3}}{2}$

(D) $2\sqrt{3}$

(E) $\dfrac{5 + 2\sqrt{3}}{2}$

19. Circle C_1 has its center O lying on circle C_2. The two circles meet at X and Y. Point Z in the exterior of C_1 lies on circle C_2 and $XZ = 13$, $OZ = 11$, and $YZ = 7$. What is the radius of circle C_1?

(A) 5

(B) $\sqrt{26}$

(C) $3\sqrt{3}$

(D) $2\sqrt{7}$

(E) $\sqrt{30}$

20. Let $ABCD$ be a cyclic quadrilateral. The side lengths of $ABCD$ are distinct integers less than 15 such that $BC \cdot CD = AB \cdot DA$. What is the largest possible value of BD?

(A) $\sqrt{\dfrac{325}{2}}$

(B) $\sqrt{185}$

(C) $\sqrt{\dfrac{389}{2}}$

(D) $\sqrt{\dfrac{425}{2}}$

(E) $\sqrt{\dfrac{533}{2}}$

21. In quadrilateral $ABCD$, it is given that $\angle A = 120°$, angles B and D are right angles, $AB = 13$, and $AD = 46$. Then $AC =$

(A) 60

(B) 62

(C) 64

(D) 65

(E) 72

187

22. The angles in a particular triangle are in arithmetic progression, and the side lengths are $4, 5, x$. The sum of the possible values of x equals $a + \sqrt{b} + \sqrt{c}$ where a, b, and c are positive integers. What is $a + b + c$?

(A) 36

(B) 38

(C) 40

(D) 42

(E) 44

23. Let C_1 and C_2 be externally tangent circles with radius 2 and 3, respectively. Let C_3 be a circle internally tangent to both C_1 and C_2 at points A and B, respectively. The tangents to C_3 at A and B meet at T, and $TA = 4$. What is the radius of C_3?

(A) 6

(B) 7

(C) 8

(D) 9

(E) 10

24. Let $\triangle ABC$ be a triangle with $AB=7$, $BC=8$, and $AC=9$. Point D is on side $\overline{AC}$ such that $\angle CBD$ has measure $45°$. What is the length of $\overline{BD}$?

(A) $40\sqrt{2}-16\sqrt{10}$

(B) $40\sqrt{3}-16\sqrt{10}$

(C) $80-16\sqrt{10}$

(D) $40\sqrt{2}-16\sqrt{5}$

(E) $40\sqrt{2}$

25. A quadrilateral is inscribed in a circle of radius $200\sqrt{2}$. Three of the sides of this quadrilateral have length 200. What is the length of the fourth side?

(A) 200

(B) $200\sqrt{2}$

(C) $200\sqrt{3}$

(D) $300\sqrt{2}$

(E) 500

26. *A* is the center of a semicircle, with radius *AD* lying on the base. *B* lies on the base between *A* and *D*, and *E* is on the circular portion of the semicircle such that *EBA* is a right angle. Extend *EA* through *A* to *C*, and put *F* on line *CD* such that *EBF* is a line.

Now $EA = 1$, $AC = \sqrt{2}$, $BF = \dfrac{2 - \sqrt{2}}{4}$, $CF = \dfrac{2\sqrt{5} + \sqrt{10}}{4}$, $DF = \dfrac{2\sqrt{5} - \sqrt{10}}{4}$.

What is the value of *DE*?

(A) $\sqrt{2 - \sqrt{2}}$

(B) $\sqrt{2 - \sqrt{3}}$

(C) $\sqrt{2}$

(D) $\sqrt{3}$

(E) $\sqrt{5}$

27. In the figure, *ABCD* is a square of side length 1. The rectangles *JKHG* and *EBCF* are congruent. What is *BE*?

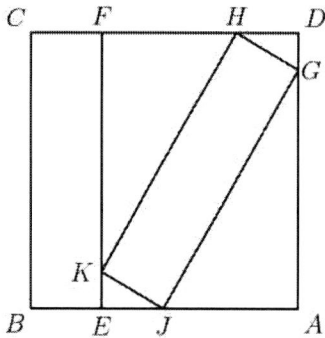

(A) $\dfrac{1}{2}(\sqrt{6} - 2)$

(B) $\dfrac{1}{4}$

(C) $2 - \sqrt{3}$

(D) $\dfrac{\sqrt{3}}{6}$

(E) $1 - \dfrac{\sqrt{2}}{2}$

190

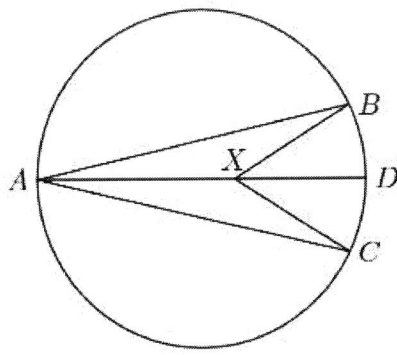

28. Points A, B, C, and D are on a circle of diameter 1, and X is on diameter $\overline{AD}$. If $BX = CX$ and $3\angle BAC = \angle BXC = 36°$, then $AX =$

(A) $\cos(6°)\cos(12°)\sec(18°)$

(B) $\cos(6°)\sin(12°)\csc(18°)$

(C) $\cos(6°)\sin(12°)\sec(18°)$

(D) $\sin(6°)\sin(12°)\csc(18°)$

(E) $\sin(6°)\sin(12°)\sec(18°)$

29. Equiangular hexagon $ABCDEF$ has side lengths $AB = CD = EF = 1$ and $BC = DE = FA = r$. The area of $\triangle ACE$ is 70% of the area of the hexagon. What is the sum of all possible values of r?

(A) $\dfrac{4\sqrt{3}}{3}$

(B) $\dfrac{10}{3}$

(C) 4

(D) $\dfrac{17}{4}$

(E) 6

30. Circles with centers $(2, 4)$ and $(14, 9)$ have radii 4 and 9, respectively. The equation of a common external tangent to the circles can be written in the form $y = mx + b$ with $m > 0$. What is b?

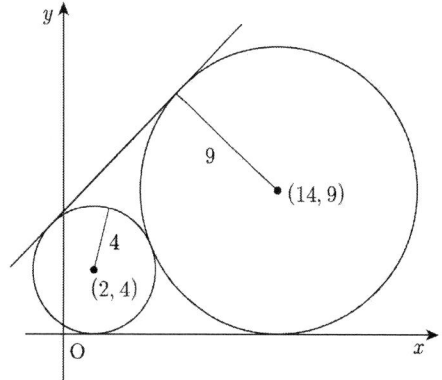

(A) $\dfrac{908}{199}$

(B) $\dfrac{908}{119}$

(C) $\dfrac{130}{17}$

(D) $\dfrac{911}{119}$

(E) $\dfrac{912}{119}$

31. In triangle ABC, side AC and the perpendicular bisector of BC meet in point D, and BD bisects $\angle ABC$. If $AD = 9$ and $DC = 7$, what is the area of triangle ABD?

(A) 14

(B) 21

(C) 28

(D) $14\sqrt{5}$

(E) $28\sqrt{5}$

32. Triangle ABC has $\angle C = 60°$ and $BC = 4$. Point D is the midpoint of BC. What is the largest possible value of $\tan \angle BAD$?

(A) $\dfrac{\sqrt{3}}{6}$

(B) $\dfrac{\sqrt{3}}{3}$

(C) $\dfrac{\sqrt{3}}{2\sqrt{2}}$

(D) $\dfrac{\sqrt{3}}{4\sqrt{2}-3}$

(E) 1

33. Isosceles $\triangle ABC$ has a right angle at C. Point P is inside $\triangle ABC$, such that $PA = 11$, $PB = 7$, and $PC = 6$. Legs $\overline{AC}$ and $\overline{BC}$ have length $s = \sqrt{a+b\sqrt{2}}$, where a and b are positive integers. What is $a+b$?

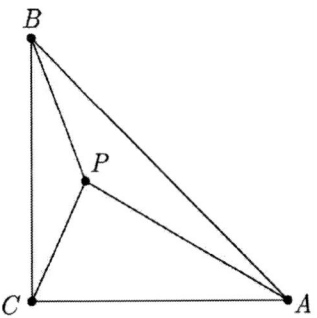

(A) 85

(B) 91

(C) 108

(D) 121

(E) 127

193

34. In $\triangle ABC$, $AB = BC$, and $\overline{BD}$ is an altitude. Point E is on the extension of $\overline{AC}$ such that $BE = 10$. The values of $\tan \angle CBE$, $\tan \angle DBE$, and $\tan \angle ABE$ form a geometric progression, and the values of $\cot \angle DBE$, $\cot \angle CBE$, $\cot \angle DBC$ form an arithmetic progression. What is the area of $\triangle ABC$?

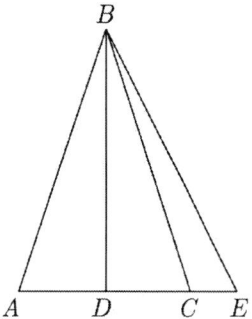

(A) 16

(B) $\dfrac{50}{3}$

(C) $10\sqrt{3}$

(D) $8\sqrt{5}$

(E) 18

Chapter 11

➢Plane Geometry 3

1. 메네라우스의 정리 (Menelaus Theorem)

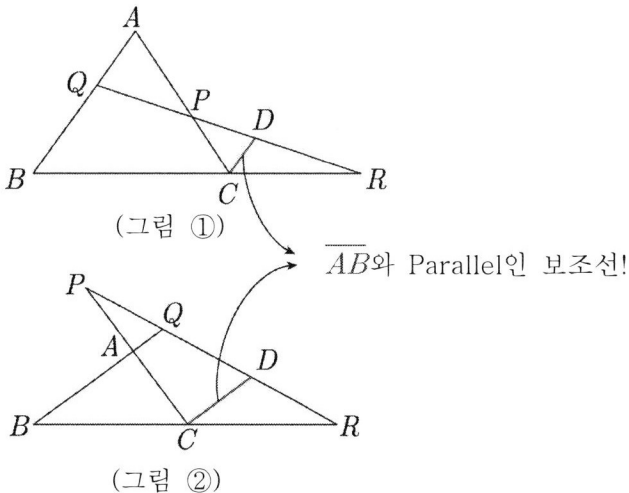

(그림 ①)

$\overline{AB}$와 Parallel인 보조선!

(그림 ②)

(그림 ①)과 (그림 ②)로 부터.....

① $\triangle DCR \backsim \triangle QBR$에서 $\dfrac{DC}{QB} = \dfrac{RC}{BR}$에서 $DC = \dfrac{RC \cdot QB}{BR}$

② $\triangle PDC \backsim \triangle PQA$에서 $\dfrac{CD}{AQ} = \dfrac{CP}{AP}$에서 $DC = \dfrac{AQ \cdot CP}{PA}$

①과 ②로부터

$\dfrac{RC \cdot QB}{BR} = \dfrac{AQ \cdot CP}{PA}$에서 $RC \cdot QB \cdot PA = AQ \cdot CP \cdot BR$로 부터

다음의 "Menelaus Theorem"이 성립한다.

$$\frac{QA}{QB} \times \frac{RB}{RC} \times \frac{CP}{AP} = 1$$

⇒ " P, Q, R 은 한 직선 위에 있다!"

2. 슈튜워드의 정리 (Stewart's theorem)

(그림 ①)

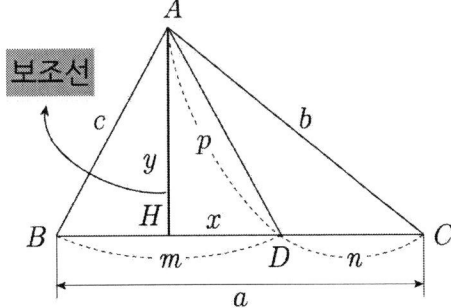

Proof ①

① $\triangle ABH$에서 $\quad c^2 = (m-x)^2 + y^2 = m^2 - 2mx + \underbrace{x^2 + y^2}_{= p^2}$

② $\triangle ACH$에서 $\quad b^2 = (n+x)^2 + y^2 = n^2 + 2nx + \underbrace{x^2 + y^2}_{= p^2}$

① $\times n +$ ②$\times m$를 하면,

$$b^2 m + c^2 m = m^2 n + np^2 + n^2 m + mp^2$$
$$= (m+n)(mn+p^2) = a(mn+p^2)$$

그러므로, 다음과 같은 "Stewart's Theorem" 이 성립한다.

$$\boxed{b^2 m + c^2 n = a(p^2 + mn)}$$

Proof ②

$\cos \angle ADB + \cos \angle ADC = 0$에서 "Law of cosine" 적용!

$$\frac{p^2 + (\frac{m}{m+n})^2 \cdot a^2 - c^2}{P \cdot \frac{m}{m+n} a} + \frac{P^2 + (\frac{n}{m+n})^2 \cdot a^2 - b^2}{P \cdot \frac{n}{m+n} a} = 0 \quad \text{을 정리하면}$$

$(m+n)p^2 + \dfrac{a^2 mn}{m+n} = mb^2 + nc^2$ 에서 $m+n = a$ 이므로

$$\boxed{a(p^2 + mn) = mb^2 + nc^2}$$

3. 파푸스의 중선정리 (Pappus's Median Theroem)

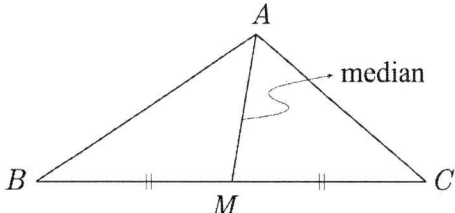

Stewart's Theorem에 의해

$$\overset{=MC}{MC \cdot AB^2 + \underset{}{\overset{}{\textcircled{BM}}} \cdot AC^2} = \overset{=2MC}{\textcircled{BC}(AM^2 + MB \cdot MC)}$$ 에서 양변을 MC로

나누면... $\boxed{AB^2 + AC^2 = 2(AM^2 + MB^2)}$

4. 톨레미의 정리 (Ptolemy's Theorem)

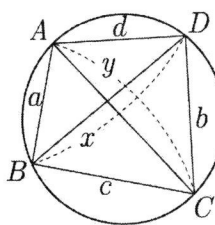

$$xy = ab + cd$$

(Proof)

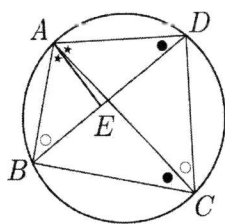

① $\overline{BD}$ 위에 $\angle BAE = \angle CAD$인 점 E와 A를 연결!

② $\triangle ABE \backsim \triangle ACD$에서 $AB : BE = AC : CD$

$\Rightarrow BE \cdot AC = AB \cdot CD$ - ⓐ

③ $\triangle ABC \backsim \triangle AED$에서 $BC : CA = ED : DA$

$\Rightarrow ED \cdot CA = DA \cdot BC$ - ⓑ

why?
- $\angle BAC = \angle EAD$ 이고 $\angle BCA = \angle BDA$ 이므로!

$\Rightarrow$ ⓐ+ⓑ $BE \cdot AC + ED \cdot CA = AB \cdot CD + DA \cdot BC$ 이므로

$BD \cdot AC = AB \cdot CD + DA \cdot BC$

199

5. 방멱정리 (Power Theorem)

①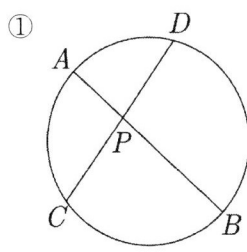

$\triangle PAD \backsim \triangle PCB\,(AA)$
$\Rightarrow\ PA:PD=PC:PB$에서
$\qquad PA\cdot PB=PC\cdot PD$

②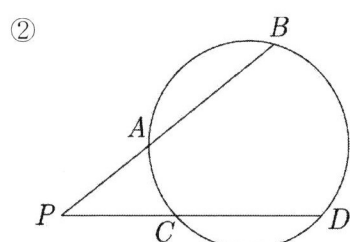

$\triangle PAD \backsim \triangle PCB$
$\Rightarrow\ PA:PD=PC:PB$에서
$\qquad PA\cdot PB=PC\cdot PD$

③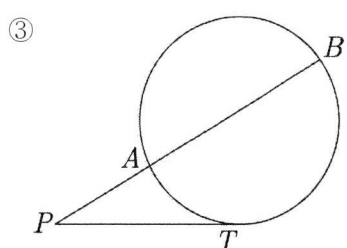

$\triangle PAT \backsim \triangle PTB\,(AA)$
($※\ \angle P$ 공통, $\angle PTA=\angle PBT$)
$\Rightarrow\ PA:PT=PT:PB$에서
$\qquad PT^{2}=PA\cdot PB$

6. 각의 이등분 정리 (The Angle Bisector Theorem)

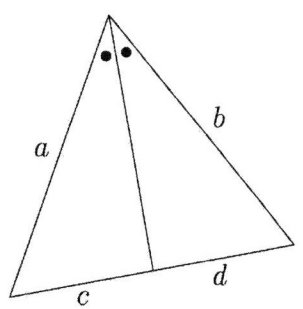

$\Rightarrow\ a:b=c:d$

다음을 보자.

높이가 같은 모든 삼각형의 Area 비는 Base 길의 비에 비례!

다음의 예를 보자.

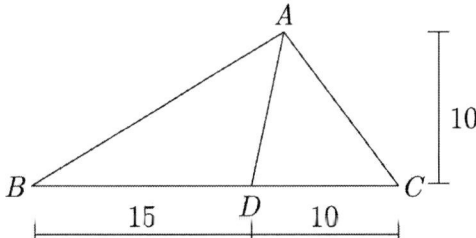

① $\triangle ABD = \dfrac{1}{2} \cdot 10 \cdot 15 = 75$

② $\triangle ACD = \dfrac{1}{2} \cdot 10 \cdot 10 = 50$

$\Rightarrow \triangle ABD : \triangle ACD = \overline{BC} : \overline{DC} = 3 : 2$

2. 위의 내용을 다음과 같이 해석할 수 있다.

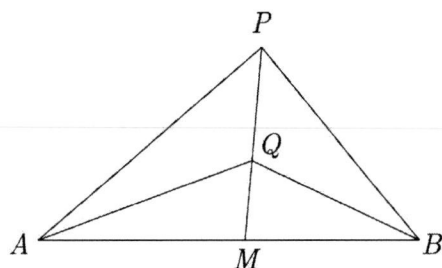

$$\frac{\triangle ABP}{\triangle ABQ} = \frac{\triangle ABP}{\triangle AMP} \cdot \frac{\triangle AMP}{\triangle AMQ} \cdot \frac{\triangle AMQ}{\triangle ABQ} = \frac{\overline{AB}}{\overline{AM}} \cdot \frac{\overline{MP}}{\overline{MQ}} \cdot \frac{\overline{AM}}{\overline{AB}} = \frac{\overline{MP}}{\overline{MQ}}$$

그러므로, $\dfrac{\triangle ABP}{\triangle ABQ} = \dfrac{\overline{PM}}{\overline{QM}}$이 성립!

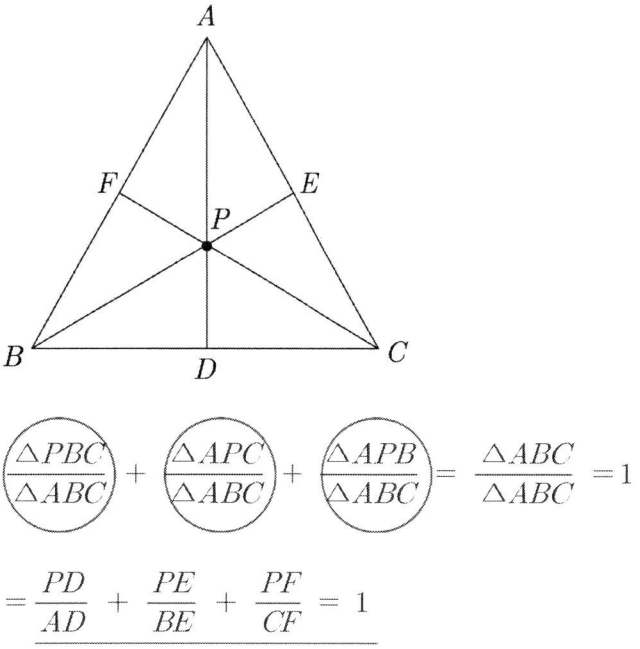

$$\left(\frac{\triangle PBC}{\triangle ABC}\right) + \left(\frac{\triangle APC}{\triangle ABC}\right) + \left(\frac{\triangle APB}{\triangle ABC}\right) = \frac{\triangle ABC}{\triangle ABC} = 1$$

$$= \frac{PD}{AD} + \frac{PE}{BE} + \frac{PF}{CF} = 1$$

이와 같은 정리를 "제르곤의 정리 (Gergonne's Theorem)"이라 한다.

7. 제르곤의 정리 (Gergonne's Theorem)

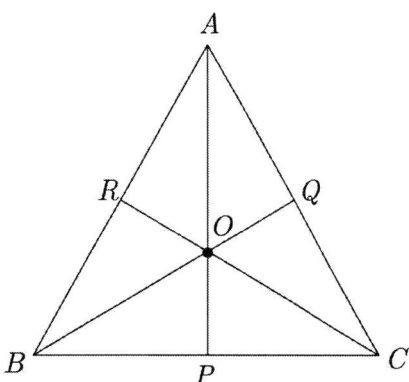

$$\frac{OP}{AP} + \frac{OQ}{BQ} + \frac{OR}{CR} = 1$$

8. 체바의 정리 (Ceva's Theorem)

$\triangle ABC$ 의 세 번 BC, CA, AB 위에 각각 주어진
점 D, E, F 에 대해서 AD, BE, CF가 한 점에서 만날 조건은

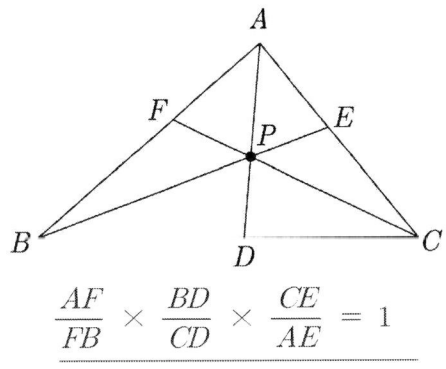

$$\frac{AF}{FB} \times \frac{BD}{CD} \times \frac{CE}{AE} = 1$$

① $\dfrac{BD}{CD} = \dfrac{\triangle ABD}{\triangle ADC} = \dfrac{\triangle PBD}{\triangle PDC} = \dfrac{\triangle ABD - \triangle PBD}{\triangle ADC - \triangle PDC} = \dfrac{\triangle APB}{\triangle APC}$

② $\dfrac{AE}{CE} = \dfrac{\triangle ABE}{\triangle BCE} = \dfrac{\triangle APE}{\triangle CPE} = \dfrac{\triangle ABE - \triangle APE}{\triangle BCE - \triangle CPE} = \dfrac{\triangle APB}{\triangle BPC}$

③ $\dfrac{BF}{AF} = \dfrac{\triangle BFC}{\triangle AFC} = \dfrac{\triangle BFP}{\triangle AFP} = \dfrac{\triangle BFC - \triangle BFP}{\triangle AFC - \triangle AFP} = \dfrac{\triangle BPC}{\triangle APC}$

① ② ③ 으로부터 "Ceva's Theorem"이 성립한다.

$$\left(\frac{\triangle APB}{\triangle APC}\right) \times \left(\frac{\triangle BPC}{\triangle APB}\right) \times \left(\frac{\triangle APC}{\triangle BPC}\right) = 1$$

$$= \boxed{\frac{BD}{CD} \times \frac{CE}{AE} + \frac{AF}{BF} = 1} \quad \text{: 체바의 정리}$$
$$\text{(Ceva's Theorem)}$$

Ceva's Theorem을 다음과 같이 해석할 수 있다.

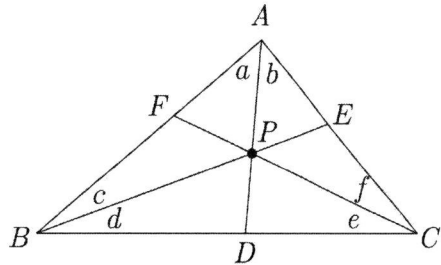

⇒ <u>Law of sine!</u>

① $\dfrac{BP}{\sin a} = \dfrac{AP}{\sin c}$ 에서 $\dfrac{\sin c}{\sin a} = \dfrac{AP}{BP}$

② $\dfrac{CP}{\sin b} = \dfrac{AP}{\sin f}$ 에서 $\dfrac{\sin f}{\sin b} = \dfrac{AP}{CP}$

③ $\dfrac{CP}{\sin d} = \dfrac{BP}{\sin e}$ 에서 $\dfrac{\sin e}{\sin d} = \dfrac{BP}{CP}$

위의 ①, ②, ③ 으로부터...

$$\left(\dfrac{AP}{BP}\right) \times \left(\dfrac{CP}{AP}\right) \times \left(\dfrac{BP}{CP}\right) = 1$$

$$= \boxed{\dfrac{\sin c}{\sin a} \times \dfrac{\sin b}{\sin f} \times \dfrac{\sin e}{\sin d}} = 1$$

01. In the figure below, if ∠BAC= ∠BDC, what is the length of $\overline{AC}$?

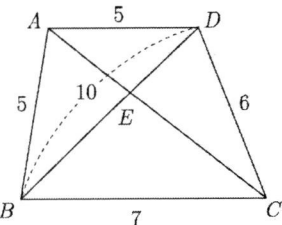

02. In the figure below, if ∠BAD= ∠BCD=90°, what is the length of diameter?

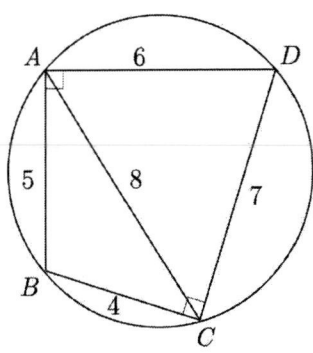

03. If the median $\overline{AM} = 8$ and $\overline{BM} = 3$, what is the length of $\overline{AB}$?

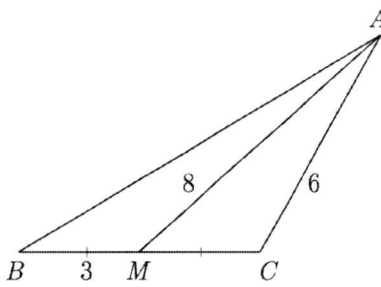

04. If F is the midpoint of $\overline{BC}$, $\overline{AC} = 4$, and $\overline{BE} : \overline{ED} = 2 : 1$, what is the length of $\overline{AD}$?

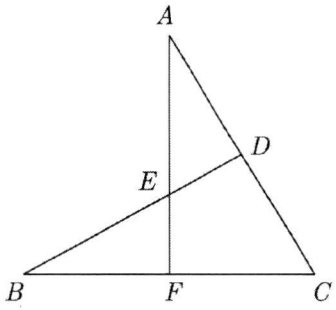

01. Triangle ABC has a right angle at B, $AB=1$, and $BC=2$. The bisector of $\angle BAC$ meets $\overline{BC}$ at D. What is BD?

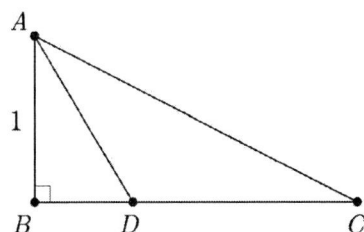

(A) $\dfrac{\sqrt{3}-1}{2}$

(B) $\dfrac{\sqrt{5}-1}{2}$

(C) $\dfrac{\sqrt{5}+1}{2}$

(D) $\dfrac{\sqrt{6}+\sqrt{2}}{2}$

(E) $2\sqrt{3}-1$

02. A, B, C, and D are points on a circle, and segments $\overline{AC}$ and $\overline{BD}$ intersect at P, such that $AP=8$, $PC=1$, and $BD=6$. Find BP, given that $BP<DP$.

(A) 1

(B) 2

(C) 3

(D) 4

(E) 5

03. Triangle ABC has side-lengths $AB=12$, $BC=24$, and $AC=18$. The line through the incenter of $\triangle ABC$ parallel to $\overline{BC}$ intersects $\overline{AB}$ at M and AC at N. What is the perimeter of $\triangle AMN$?

(A) 27

(B) 30

(C) 33

(D) 36

(E) 42

04. Circle C_1 has its center O lying on circle C_2. The two circles meet at X and Y. Point Z in the exterior of C_1 lies on circle C_2 and $XZ=13$, $OZ=11$, and $YZ=7$. What is the radius of circle C_1?

(A) 5

(B) $\sqrt{26}$

(C) $3\sqrt{3}$

(D) $2\sqrt{7}$

(E) $\sqrt{30}$

05. Point D is drawn on side BC of equilateral triangle ABC, and AD is extended past D to E such that angles EAC and EBC are equal. If $BE=5$ and $CE=12$, What is the length of AE?

(A) 16

(B) 17

(C) 17.5

(D) 18

(E) 19.5

06. Convex quadrilateral $ABCD$ has sides $AB=BC=7$, $CD=5$, and $AD=3$. Given additionally that $\angle ABC=60°$, What is the length of $\overline{BD}$?

(A) 6.5

(B) 7

(C) 7.5

(D) 8

(E) 9

07. In $\triangle ABC$, $AB=86$, and $AC=97$. A circle with center A and radius AB intersects $\overline{BC}$ at points B and X. Moreover $\overline{BX}$ and $\overline{CX}$ have integer lengths. What is BC?

(A) 11

(B) 28

(C) 33

(D) 61

(E) 72

08. In $\triangle ABC$, we have $AB=1$ and $AC=2$. Side $\overline{BC}$ and the median from A to $\overline{BC}$ have the same length. What is BC?

(A) $\dfrac{1+\sqrt{2}}{2}$

(B) $\dfrac{1+\sqrt{3}}{2}$

(C) $\sqrt{2}$

(D) $\dfrac{3}{2}$

(E) $\sqrt{3}$

09. In $\triangle ABC$, D is the midpoint of BC, E is the foot of the perpendicular from A to BC, and F is the foot of the perpendicular from D to AC. Given that $BE=5$, $EC=9$, and the area of triangle ABC is 84, What is $|EF|$?

(A) $\dfrac{6\sqrt{37}}{5}$

(B) $\dfrac{3\sqrt{33}}{5}$

(C) $\sqrt{35}$

(D) $\dfrac{\sqrt{33}}{3}$

(E) 7

10. Let A, B, C, and D be points on a circle such that $AB=11$ and $CD=19$. Point P is on segment AB with $AP=6$, and Q is on segment CD with $CQ=7$. The line through P and Q intersects the circle at X and Y. If $PQ=27$, find XY.

(A) 30

(B) 31

(C) 32

(D) 33

(E) 34

11. Let ABC be a triangle where M is the midpoint of $\overline{AC}$, and $\overline{CN}$ is the angle bisector of $\angle ACB$ with N on $\overline{AB}$. Let X be the intersection of the median $\overline{BM}$ and the bisector $\overline{CN}$. In addition $\triangle BXN$ is equilateral with $AC=2$. What is BN^2?

(A) $\dfrac{10-6\sqrt{2}}{7}$

(B) $\dfrac{2}{9}$

(C) $\dfrac{5\sqrt{2}-3\sqrt{3}}{8}$

(D) $\dfrac{\sqrt{2}}{6}$

(E) $\dfrac{3\sqrt{3}-4}{5}$

12. Points A and B lie on circle C. Point P lies on the extension of segment AB past B. Line l passes through P and is tangent to C. The tangents to C at points A and B intersect l at points D and C respectively. Given that $AB=7$, $BC=2$, and $AD=3$, what is BP?

(A) 6.5
(B) 7
(C) 7.5
(D) 8
(E) 8.5

13. Given noncollinear points A, B, C, segment $\overline{AB}$ is trisected by points D and E, and F is the midpoint of segment $\overline{AC}$. $\overline{DF}$ and $\overline{BF}$ intersect $\overline{CE}$ at G and H, respectively. If area of $\triangle GDE$ is 18, what is the area of $\triangle FGH$?

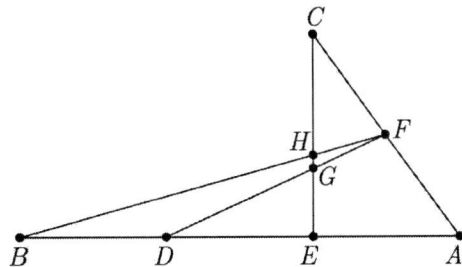

(A) 1

(B) $\dfrac{9}{5}$

(C) 2

(D) $\dfrac{11}{5}$

(E) 3

14. Let $ABCDE$ be a pentagon inscribed in a circle such that $AB = CD = 3$, $BC = DE = 10$, and $AE = 14$. The sum of the lengths of all diagonals of $ABCDE$ is equal to $\dfrac{m}{n}$, where m and n are relatively prime positive integers.

What is $m+n$?

(A) 129

(B) 247

(C) 353

(D) 391

(E) 421

15. The diameter AB of a circle of radius 2 is extended to a point D outside the circle so that $BD=3$. Point E is chosen so that $ED=5$ and line ED is perpendicular to line AD. Segment AE intersects the circle at a point C between A and E. What is the area of $\triangle ABC$?

(A) $\dfrac{120}{37}$

(B) $\dfrac{140}{39}$

(C) $\dfrac{145}{39}$

(D) $\dfrac{140}{37}$

(E) $\dfrac{120}{31}$

16. In triangle ABC, $AB=13$, $BC=14$, $AC=15$. Let D denote the midpoint of $\overline{BC}$ and let E denote the intersection of $\overline{BC}$ with the bisector of angle BAC. Which of the following is closest to the area of the triangle ADE?

(A) 2
(B) 2.5
(C) 3
(D) 3.5
(E) 4

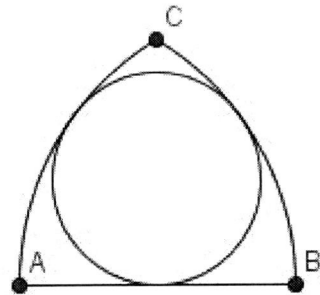

17. If circular arcs AC and BC have centers at B and A, respectively, then there exists a circle tangent to both $\overset{\frown}{AC}$ and $\overset{\frown}{BC}$, and to $\overline{AB}$. If the length of $\overset{\frown}{BC}$ is 12, then the circumference of the circle is

(A) 24

(B) 25

(C) 26

(D) 27

(E) 28

읽을거리

걸리버의 식료품과 식사

〈걸리버 여행기〉를 읽으면 소인국의 릴리파트 인은 걸리버에게 지급하는 식료품의 기준량을 다음과 같이 정했다.

「……그에게는 매일 릴리파트 인의 1728 명분의 식량과 음료수를 지급한다.」

또, 걸리버는 이렇게 이야기하고 있다. ―「……300인의 요리사가 나를 위해 음식을 만들었다. 내 집의 주위에는 조그만 집이 지어졌고 그 곳에서 취사를 하고 요리사를 하고 요리사들도 가족과 함께 거기에 살았다. 식사 때에 나는 20명의 하인들을 식탁 위에 올려놓아 주었다. 그러자 바닥에 있는 100명 정도의 하인들이 대기하고 있으면서 어떤 사람은 음식물이 담긴 접시를 올리고, 어떤 사람들은 포도주나 그 밖의 통을 서로 어깨에서 어깨로 걸친 나무 봉으로 운반했다. 위에 있는 하인들은 내가 원하기만 하면 무엇이든 밧줄과 도르래로 식탁 위에 끌어 올려놓았다.……」

그런데 릴리파트 인들은 어떤 계산에서 이렇게 많은 음식물의 양을 정했을까?

또, 한 사람의 인간에게 음식을 주는 데 어떻게 이렇게 많은 하인들이 필요했을까?

걸리버는 키가 큰 릴리파트 인보다 고작 해서 12배밖에 크지 않았다. 걸리버가 먹는 음식물의 양도 식욕도 릴리파트 인의 12배가 큰 것이었을까?

풀이

그와 같은 계산은 아주 옳은 것이다. 릴리파트 인의 키는 걸리버의 키의 12분의 1이지만 부피도 12분의 1이라는 것은 아니고 부피는 1728(=12×12×12)분의 1이 된다. 릴리파트 인보다 12배 큰 걸리버는 생명을 유지하기 위해 그에 어울리는 식량을 취하지 않으면 안 된다. 따라서 릴리파트 인은 걸리버에게 자기들의 1728명분에 해당하는 음식이 필요하다고 계산을 한 것이다.

여기서 걸리버를 위해서 그렇게 많은 요리사가 필요했다는 것도 이해할 수 있다. 1728명분의 요리를 만드는 데는 한 사람의 릴리파트 인의 요리사가 릴리파트 인 6인분의 요리를 만들 수 있다고 해도 적어도 300명은 필요했을 것이다. 따라서 하인이 100명 정도 있었다는 것도 납득할 수 있다.

Chapter 12

➤Space Geometry

Space Geometry

"Space Geometry" 즉, 공간도형 문제는 대부분의 학생들이 막연하게 생각하는 단원이다. 공간도형 문제도 풀이 방법과 이론이 있음에도 이를 활용하지 못하고 무조건 어렵다고만 생각을 한다.

다음에 설명하는 내용들을 익힌 후 문제들을 통해서 자세한 사항들을 알아두도록 하자.

1. Dihedral Angle

두 면이 이루는 각(Angle)을 말하며 그림과 같이 면과 면이 만나서 생기는 선(Line)과 수직(Perpendicular)이 되어야 한다.

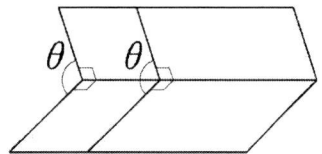

2. Theorem of three perpendiculars

Space 상에서 Plane을 수직으로 지나는 선(Line)이 있을 때 세 개의 선(Line)으로 직각 삼각형(Right Triangle)을 만드는 이론이다.

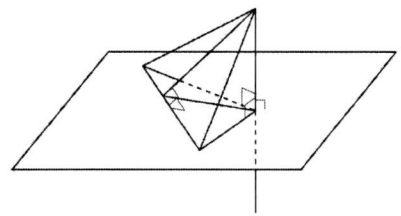

3. Equation

① Plane : $ax + by + cz + d = 0$

② Sphere : $(x-a)^2 + (y-b)^2 + (z-c)^2 = r^2$

$\Rightarrow$ • Center (a, b, c) • Radius : r

4. Distance

①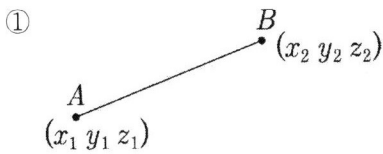

$$\overline{AB} = \sqrt{(x_2 - x_1)^2 + (y_2 - y_1)^2 + (z_2 - z_1)^2}$$

②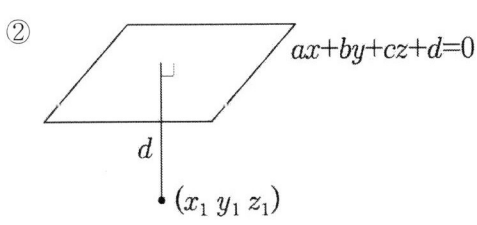

$$d = \frac{|ax_1 + by_1 + cz_1 + d|}{\sqrt{a^2 + b^2 + c^2}}$$

5. Internal Division Point

·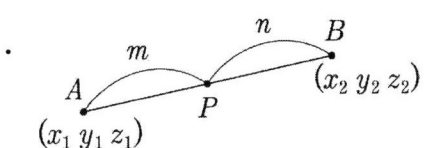

$$P\left(\frac{mx_2 + nx_1}{m+n}, \ \frac{my_2 + ny_1}{m+n}, \ \frac{mz_2 + nz_1}{m+n}\right)$$

· Midpoint

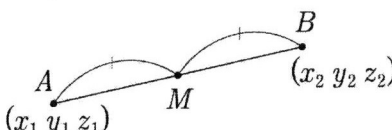

$$M\left(\frac{x_1 + x_2}{2}, \ \frac{y_1 + y_2}{2}, \ \frac{z_1 + z_2}{2}\right)$$

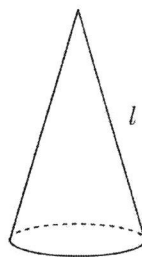

01. The cone above has an altitude of b and a base circle with an area of $4\pi a^2$. If $a = b$, then what is the length of l ?

   (A) a

   (B) $\sqrt{3}\,a$

   (C) $2a$

   (D) $\sqrt{5}\,a$

   (E) $3a$

02. The area of the base of a pyramid is 2×2 and the altitude is $\sqrt{3}$. Then what is the dihedral angle between base and lateral side of this pyramid?

   (A) $15°$

   (B) $30°$

   (C) $45°$

   (D) $60°$

   (E) $90°$

03. On a $4 \times 4 \times 3$ rectangular parallelepiped, vertices A, B, and C are adjacent to vertex D. The perpendicular distance from D to the plane containing A, B, and C is closest to

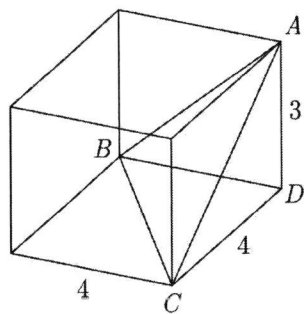

(A) 1.6

(B) 1.9

(C) 2.1

(D) 2.7

(E) 2.9

04. The circular base of a hemisphere of radius 2 rests on the base of a square pyramid of height 6. The hemisphere is tangent to the other four faces of the pyramid. What is the edge-length of the base of the pyramid?

(A) $3\sqrt{2}$

(B) $\dfrac{13}{3}$

(C) $4\sqrt{2}$

(D) 6

(E) $\dfrac{13}{2}$

05. Three mutually tangent spheres of radius 1 rest on a horizontal plane. A sphere of radius 2 rests on them. What is the distance from the plane to the top of the larger sphere?

(A) $3 + \dfrac{\sqrt{30}}{2}$

(B) $3 + \dfrac{\sqrt{69}}{3}$

(C) $3 + \dfrac{\sqrt{123}}{4}$

(D) $\dfrac{52}{9}$

(E) $3 + 2\sqrt{2}$

06. Triangle ABC, with sides of length 5, 6, and 7, has one vertex on the positive x−axis, one on the positive y−axis, and one on the positive z−axis. Let O be the origin. What is the volume of tetrahedron $OABC$?

(A) $\sqrt{85}$

(B) $\sqrt{90}$

(C) $\sqrt{95}$

(D) 10

(E) $\sqrt{105}$

07. A pyramid has a square base $ABCD$ and vertex E. The area of square $ABCD$ is 196, and the areas of $\triangle ABE$ and $\triangle CDE$ are 105 and 91, respectively. What is the volume of the pyramid?

(A) 392

(B) $196\sqrt{6}$

(C) $392\sqrt{2}$

(D) $392\sqrt{3}$

(E) 784

08. A cylindrical tank with radius 4 feet and height 9 feet is lying on its side. The tank is filled with water to a depth of 2 feet. What is the volume of water, in cubic feet?

(A) $24\pi - 36\sqrt{2}$

(B) $24\pi - 24\sqrt{3}$

(C) $36\pi - 36\sqrt{3}$

(D) $36\pi - 24\sqrt{2}$

(E) $48\pi - 36\sqrt{3}$

09. A pyramid has a square base with sides of length 1 and has lateral faces that are equilateral triangles. A cube is placed within the pyramid so that one face is on the base of the pyramid and its opposite face has all its edges on the lateral faces of the pyramid. What is the volume of this cube?

(A) $5\sqrt{2}-7$

(B) $7-4\sqrt{3}$

(C) $\dfrac{2\sqrt{2}}{27}$

(D) $\dfrac{\sqrt{2}}{9}$

(E) $\dfrac{\sqrt{3}}{9}$

10. A regular hexagon with sides of length 6 has an isosceles triangle attached to each side. Each of these triangles has two sides of length 8. The isosceles triangles are folded to make a pyramid with the hexagon as the base of the pyramid. What is the volume of the pyramid?

(A) 18

(B) 162

(C) $36\sqrt{21}$

(D) $18\sqrt{138}$

(E) $54\sqrt{21}$

11. Six spheres of radius 1 are positioned so that their centers are at the vertices of a regular hexagon of side length 2. The six spheres are internally tangent to a larger sphere whose center is the center of the hexagon. An eighth sphere is externally tangent to the six smaller spheres and internally tangent to the larger sphere. What is the radius of this eighth sphere?

(A) $\sqrt{2}$

(B) $\dfrac{3}{2}$

(C) $\dfrac{5}{3}$

(D) $\sqrt{3}$

(E) 2

12. Consider a pyramid $P-ABCD$ whose base $ABCD$ is square and whose vertex P is equidistant from A, B, C, and D. If $AB=1$ and $\angle APB=2\theta$, then the volume of the pyramid is

(A) $\dfrac{\sin(\theta)}{6}$

(B) $\dfrac{\cot(\theta)}{6}$

(C) $\dfrac{1}{6\sin(\theta)}$

(D) $\dfrac{1-\sin(2\theta)}{6}$

(E) $\dfrac{\sqrt{\cos(2\theta)}}{6\sin(\theta)}$

13. A $4 \times 4 \times h$ rectangular box contains a sphere of radius 2 and eight smaller spheres of radius 1. The smaller spheres are each tangent to three sides of the box, and the larger sphere is tangent to each of the smaller spheres. What is h?

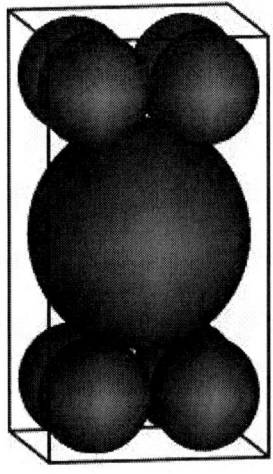

(A) $2+2\sqrt{7}$

(B) $3+2\sqrt{5}$

(C) $4+2\sqrt{7}$

(D) $4\sqrt{5}$

(E) $4\sqrt{7}$

14. A sphere is inscribed in a truncated right circular cone as shown. The volume of the truncated cone is twice that of the sphere. What is the ratio of the radius of the bottom base of the truncated cone to the radius of the top base of the truncated cone?

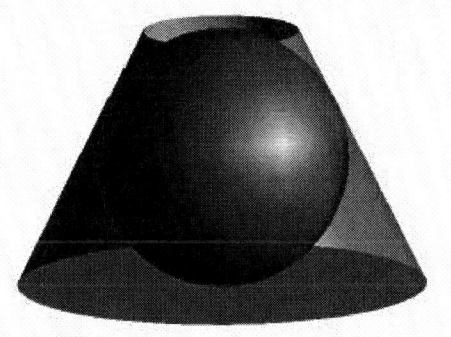

(A) $\dfrac{3}{2}$

(B) $\dfrac{1+\sqrt{5}}{2}$

(C) $\sqrt{3}$

(D) 2

(E) $\dfrac{3+\sqrt{5}}{2}$

15. Nine congruent spheres are packed inside a unit cube in such a way that one of them has its center at the center of the cube and each of the others is tangent to the center sphere and to three faces of the cube. What is the radius of each sphere?

(A) $1 - \dfrac{\sqrt{3}}{2}$

(B) $\dfrac{2\sqrt{3} - 3}{2}$

(C) $\dfrac{\sqrt{2}}{6}$

(D) $\dfrac{1}{4}$

(E) $\dfrac{\sqrt{3}\,(2 - \sqrt{2}\,)}{4}$

16. Tetrahedron $ABCD$ has $AB = 5$, $AC = 3$, $BC = 4$, $BD = 4$, $AD = 3$, and $CD = \dfrac{12}{5}\sqrt{20}$. What is the volume of the tetrahedron?

(A) $3\sqrt{2}$

(B) $2\sqrt{5}$

(C) $\dfrac{24}{5}$

(D) $3\sqrt{3}$

(E) $\dfrac{24}{5}\sqrt{2}$

Chapter 13

➤Trigonometry

Sum and Difference

· $\sin(\alpha \pm \beta) = \sin\alpha\cos\beta \pm \cos\alpha\sin\beta$

· $\cos(\alpha \pm \beta) = \cos\alpha\cos\beta \mp \sin\alpha\sin\beta$

· $\tan(\alpha \pm \beta) = \dfrac{\tan\alpha \pm \tan\beta}{1 \mp \tan\alpha \cdot \tan\beta}$

Double Angle

· $\sin2\alpha = 2\sin\alpha\cos\alpha$

· $\cos2\alpha = \cos^2\alpha - \sin^2\alpha$

$= 1 - 2\sin^2\alpha$

$= 2\cos^2\alpha - 1$

· $\tan2\alpha = \dfrac{2\tan\alpha}{1 - \tan^2\alpha}$

Power − Reduce

· $\sin^2\dfrac{\alpha}{2} = \dfrac{1 - \cos\alpha}{2}$

· $\cos^2\dfrac{\alpha}{2} = \dfrac{1 + \cos\alpha}{2}$

· $\tan^2\dfrac{\alpha}{2} = \dfrac{1 - \cos\alpha}{1 + \cos\alpha}$

Triple Angle

· $\sin3\alpha = 3\sin\alpha - 4\sin^3\alpha$

· $\cos3\alpha = 4\cos^3\alpha - 3\cos\alpha$

Sum/Difference ⇔ Product

· $\sin\alpha + \sin\beta = 2\sin\dfrac{\alpha+\beta}{2} \cdot \cos\dfrac{\alpha-\beta}{2}$

· $\sin\alpha - \sin\beta = 2\cos\dfrac{\alpha+\beta}{2} \cdot \sin\dfrac{\alpha-\beta}{2}$

· $\cos\alpha + \cos\beta = 2\cos\dfrac{\alpha+\beta}{2} \cdot \cos\dfrac{\alpha-\beta}{2}$

· $\cos\alpha - \cos\beta = -2\sin\dfrac{\alpha+\beta}{2} \cdot \sin\dfrac{\alpha-\beta}{2}$

Product ⇔ Sum/Difference

· $\sin\alpha \cdot \cos\beta = \dfrac{1}{2}\{\sin(\alpha+\beta) + \sin(\alpha-\beta)\}$

· $\cos\alpha \cdot \sin\beta = \dfrac{1}{2}\{\sin(\alpha+\beta) - \sin(\alpha-\beta)\}$

· $\cos\alpha \cdot \cos\beta = \dfrac{1}{2}\{\cos(\alpha+\beta) + \cos(\alpha-\beta)\}$

$\sin\alpha \cdot \sin\beta = -\dfrac{1}{2}\{\cos(\alpha+\beta) - \cos(\alpha-\beta)\}$

230

$\sin(\pi-\theta)=\sin\theta,$ $\sin\left(\dfrac{3}{2}\pi+\theta\right)=-\cos\theta$

$\cos(\pi-\theta)=-\cos\theta$ $\tan(\pi-\theta)=-\tan\theta$

$\sin\left(\dfrac{\pi}{2}+\theta\right)=\cos\theta$ $\tan\left(\dfrac{\pi}{2}+\theta\right)=-\cot\theta$

$\cos(2\pi-\theta)=\cos\theta$ $\sin(\pi+\theta)=-\sin\theta$ $\cdots$등등

$\boxed{\text{Sine으로 합성하기}}$

· $\sin\alpha+\sin\beta$ ⎫ 이 4가지는 Sum/Difference를
· $\sin\alpha-\sin\beta$ ⎪ 모두 Product 공식으로 바꿀 수 있다.
· $\cos\alpha+\cos\beta$ ⎬ sine끼리 $+$ $-$하든가 cosine끼리 $+$ $-$할 때...
· $\cos\alpha-\cos\beta$ ⎭ 그리고 Angle α,β로 다를 때에는 공식이 존재!

01. Suppose that $\sin a + \sin b = \sqrt{\dfrac{5}{3}}$ and $\cos a + \cos b = 1$. What is $\cos(a-b)$?

(A) $\sqrt{\dfrac{5}{3}} - 1$

(B) $\dfrac{1}{3}$

(C) $\dfrac{1}{2}$

(D) $\dfrac{2}{3}$

(E) 1

02. If $\displaystyle\sum_{n=0}^{\infty} \cos^{2n}\theta = 5$, what is the value of $\cos 2\theta$?

(A) $\dfrac{1}{5}$

(B) $\dfrac{2}{5}$

(C) $\dfrac{\sqrt{5}}{5}$

(D) $\dfrac{3}{5}$

(E) $\dfrac{4}{5}$

03. Compute the value of the sum

$$\frac{1}{1+\tan^3 0\,^\circ} + \frac{1}{1+\tan^3 10\,^\circ} + \frac{1}{1+\tan^3 20\,^\circ} + \frac{1}{1+\tan^3 30\,^\circ} + \frac{1}{1+\tan^3 40\,^\circ}$$
$$+ \frac{1}{1+\tan^3 50\,^\circ} + \frac{1}{1+\tan^3 60\,^\circ} + \frac{1}{1+\tan^3 70\,^\circ} + \frac{1}{1+\tan^3 80\,^\circ}.$$

(A) 1
(B) 2
(C) 3
(D) 4
(E) 5

04. If a and b are positive integers such that $\sqrt{8+\sqrt{32+\sqrt{768}}} = a\cos\dfrac{\pi}{b}$, what is the ordered pair (a, b) ?

(A) $(4, 24)$

(B) $(4, 20)$

(C) $(4, 16)$

(D) $(2, 24)$

(E) $(2, 20)$

05. There are real numbers a and b such that for every positive number x, we have the identity

$$\tan^{-1}(\frac{1}{x}-\frac{x}{8})+\tan^{-1}(ax)+\tan^{-1}(bx) = \frac{\pi}{2}.$$

(Throughout this equation, $\tan^{-1}$ means the inverse tangent function, sometimes written arctan. What is the value of a^2+b^2?

(A) $\dfrac{3}{4}$

(B) $\dfrac{3}{5}$

(C) $\dfrac{1}{2}$

(D) $\dfrac{1}{4}$

(E) $\dfrac{1}{8}$

06. What is the sum of all positive integer values of n that satisfy the equation

$$\cos\left(\frac{\pi}{n}\right)\cos\left(\frac{2\pi}{n}\right)\cos\left(\frac{4\pi}{n}\right)\cos\left(\frac{8\pi}{n}\right)\cos\left(\frac{16\pi}{n}\right) = \frac{1}{32}?$$

(A) 45

(B) 47

(C) 49

(D) 50

(E) 52

07. If $\sin x + \sin y = \frac{96}{65}$ and $\cos x + \cos y = \frac{72}{65}$, then what is the value of $\tan x + \tan y$?

(A) $\dfrac{507}{112}$

(B) $\dfrac{50}{11}$

(C) $\dfrac{509}{112}$

(D) 5

(E) 4

Chapter 14

➢Complex Number

Complex Number

"Complex Number"란 무엇인가?

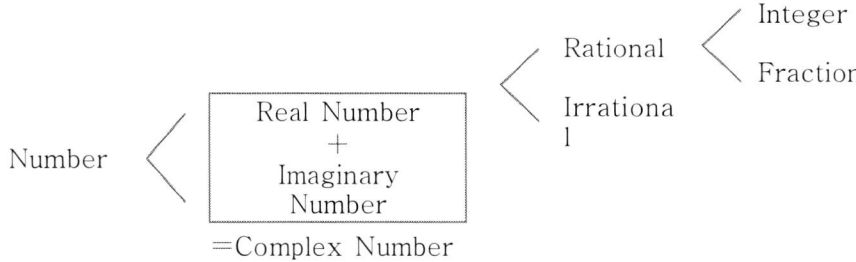

즉, Complex Number = Real Number + Imaginary Number
이므로 모든 Number를 뜻한다. 그러므로, 다음과 같이 쓰인다.

$$z = a + bi \text{(Standard Form)}$$

앞으로 Plane Coordinate에 $z = a + bi$는 (a, b)로 나타낼 수 있음을 알아두자.

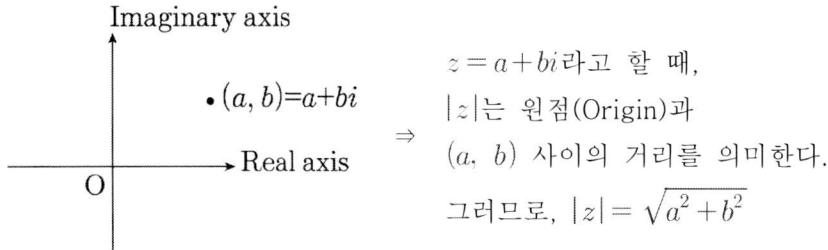

$z = a + bi$라고 할 때,
$|z|$는 원점(Origin)과
(a, b) 사이의 거리를 의미한다.
그러므로, $|z| = \sqrt{a^2 + b^2}$

앞의 그림으로부터 $\cos\theta = \dfrac{a}{r}$, $\sin\theta = \dfrac{b}{r}$ 이므로

$$z = r(\cos\theta + i\sin\theta) = r\left(\dfrac{a}{r} + i\dfrac{b}{r}\right) = a + bi$$

즉, $z = a + bi$ 를 $z = r(\cos\theta + i\sin\theta)$ 인
Trigonometric Form으로 나타낼 수 있다. 앞으로
중요하게 쓰이는 Form이므로 반드시 암기하여야 한다.

반드시 암기하자!

$$z = a + bi = r(\cos\theta + i\sin)$$

$z_1 = a + bi = r_1(\cos\theta_1 + i\sin\theta_1)$,
$z_2 = c + di = r_2(\cos\theta_2 + i\sin\theta_2)$ 라고 하면

$$\begin{aligned}
z_1 \cdot z_2 &= (a+bi)(c+di) \\
&= r_1 r_2\{\cos\theta_1\cos\theta_2 - \sin\theta_1\sin\theta_2 + i(\sin\theta_1\cos\theta_2 + \sin\theta_2\cos\theta_1\} \\
&= r_1 r_2(\cos(\theta_1 + \theta_2) + i\sin(\theta_1 + \theta_2))
\end{aligned}$$

$$\begin{aligned}
&※\ \cos(\alpha + \beta) = \cos\alpha\cos\beta - \sin\alpha\sin\beta \\
&\quad \sin(\alpha + \beta) = \sin\alpha\cos\beta + \cos\alpha\sin\beta
\end{aligned}$$

즉, $z_1, z_2 = (a+bi)(c+di) = r_1 r_2(\cos(\theta_1 + \theta_2) + i\sin(\theta_1 + \theta_2)$로부터 다음을 알 수 있다.

$z = a + bi = r(\cos\theta + i\sin\theta)$로 부터

$z^2 = (a+bi)^2 = r^2(\cos2\theta + i\sin2\theta)$

$z^3 = (a+bi)^3 = r^3(\cos3\theta + i\sin3\theta)\cdots$

$z^n = (a+bi)^n = r^n(\cos n\theta + i\sin n\theta)$

$z^n = (a+bi)^n = r^n(\cos n\theta + i \sin n\theta)$를

"DeMoivre's Theorem"이라고 한다. 반드시 암기하자!

반드시 암기하자!

DeMoivre's Theorem
$$Z^n = (a+bi)^n = r^n(\cos n\theta + i \sin n\theta)$$

앞으로 중요하게 쓰여지는 Theorem 이다.

한 가지만 예를 들어 본다면....

$z = 1 + \sqrt{3}\,i$ 라고 할때, z^6 를 구해보자.
$z^6 = (1+\sqrt{3}\,i)^6$ 을 계산할 자신이 있는가?
이런 경우 유용하게 쓰이는 이론이 바로
"DeMoivre's Theorem" 이다.

다음과 같이 "DeMoivre's Theorem" 을 이용하여
풀어 보자.

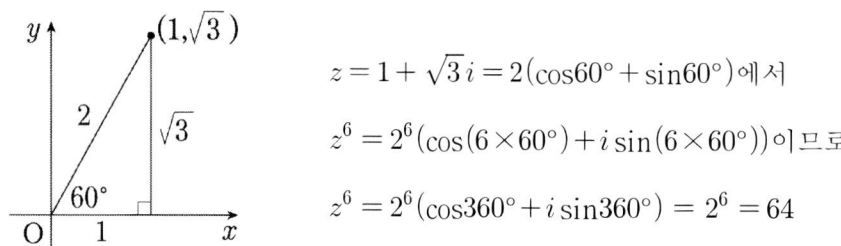

$z = 1 + \sqrt{3}\,i = 2(\cos 60° + \sin 60°)$에서

$z^6 = 2^6(\cos(6 \times 60°) + i \sin(6 \times 60°))$이므로

$z^6 = 2^6(\cos 360° + i \sin 360°) = 2^6 = 64$

참고로 시험에 자주 활용 되지는 않지만 다음의 사항도 알아두자.

$z_1 = a+bi = r_1(\cos\theta_1 + i \sin\theta_1)$, $z_2 = c+di = r_2(\cos\theta_2 + i \sin\theta_2)$ 라고 하면,
$$\frac{z_2}{z_1} = \frac{r_2(\cos\theta_2 + i \sin\theta_2)(\cos\theta_1 - i \sin\theta_1)}{r_1(\cos\theta_1 + i \sin\theta_1)(\cos\theta_1 - i \sin\theta_1)}$$ 로부터

$$\frac{z_2}{z_1} = \frac{r_2\{\cos\theta_1\cos\theta_2 + \sin\theta_1\sin\theta_2 + i(\sin\theta_1\cos\theta_2 - \cos\theta_1\sin\theta_2)\}}{r_1(\cos^2\theta_1 + \sin^2\theta_1)}$$

그러므로, $\dfrac{z_2}{z_1} = \dfrac{r_2}{r_1}(\cos(\theta_1 - \theta_2) + i\sin(\theta_1 - \theta_2))$

Roots of Complex Numbers

$x^3 = 1$에서 x값을 찾아보자.
지금까지 풀던 방식대로 해보면...

$x^3 - 1 = (x-1)(x^2 + x + 1) = 0$에서

$x = 1, \ x = \dfrac{-1 \pm \sqrt{3}\,i}{2}$

그렇다면, $x^3 = 1 + \sqrt{3}\,i$ 에서 이와 같은 방법으로
x값을 구할 수 있는가? 아마도 어려울걸?

"DeMoire's Theorem"을 이용해서 푸는 방법을
익히도록 하자. 매우 중요한 내용이니 꼭 알아 두어야 한다.

$x^3 = 1$에서 x는 All Number 이므로 Complex Number "z"로 두고 풀자.

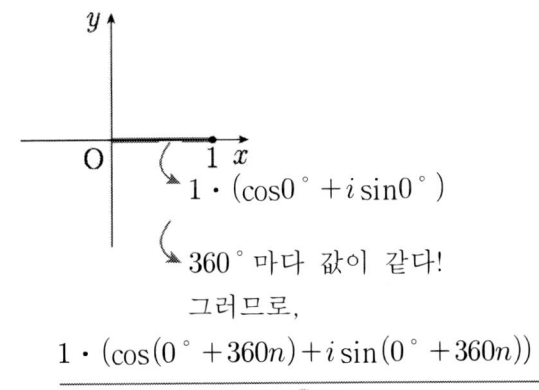

$z^3 = 1 \xrightarrow{\ 1 + 0 \cdot i = (1,\ 0)\ }$

$z = a + bi$
$z = r(\cos\theta + i\sin\theta)$
$\underset{①}{\underline{z^3 = r^3(\cos3\theta + i\sin3\theta)}}$

$1 \cdot (\cos0° + i\sin0°)$

$360°$마다 값이 같다!

그러므로,

$\underset{②}{\underline{1 \cdot (\cos(0° + 360n) + i\sin(0° + 360n))}}$

① = ②로부터,

$r^3 = 1$, $3\theta = 0° + 360n$에서 $r = 1$, $\theta = 120n$

$r = 1$, $\theta = 120n$을 $z = r(\cos\theta + i\sin\theta)$에 대입하면

$z = (\cos 120n + i\sin 120n)$에서

· $n = 0$, $z = \cos 0° + i\sin 0° = 1$

· $n = 1$, $z = \cos 120° + i\sin 120° = -\dfrac{1}{2} + \dfrac{\sqrt{3}}{2}i$

· $n = 2$, $z = \cos 240° + i\sin 240° = -\dfrac{1}{2} - \dfrac{\sqrt{3}}{2}i$

· $n = 3$이면 $z = \cos 360° + i\sin 360°$이므로 $n = 0$일 때와 값이 같다.

· $n = 0$, 1, 2 일 때의 z를 좌표에 나타내면 다음과 같다.

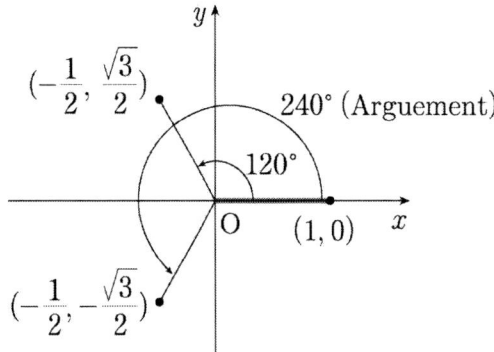

다음의 예제를 풀어보자.

(Example) Find the three cube roots
of $z = 1 + \sqrt{3}\,i$

(Solution)

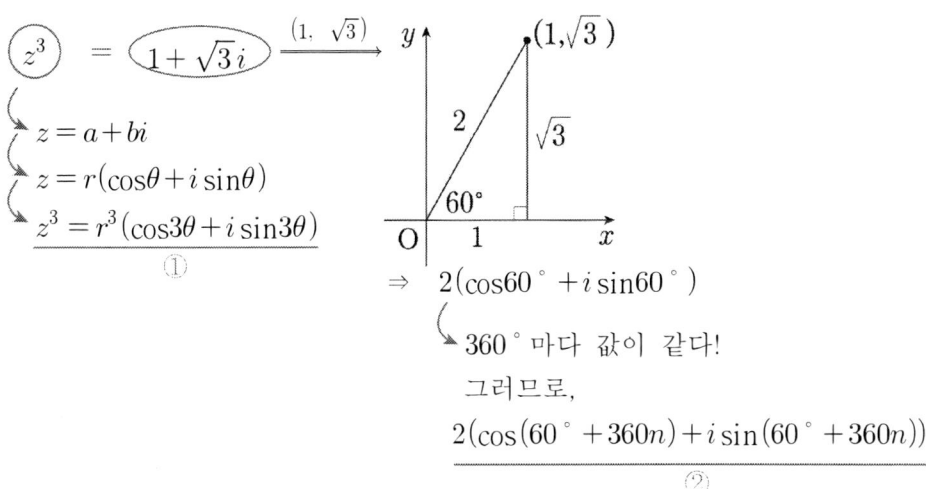

① = ②로부터

$r^3 = 2,\ 3\theta = 60° + 360n$ 에서 $r = \sqrt[3]{2},\ \theta = 20° + 120n$

$r = \sqrt[3]{2},\ \theta = 20° + 120n$ 을 $z = r(\cos\theta + i\sin\theta)$ 에 대입하면

$z = \sqrt[3]{2}\,(\cos(20° + 120n) + i\sin(20° + 120n))$ 에서

· $n = 0,\ z = \sqrt[3]{2}\,(\cos20° + i\sin20°)$

· $n = 1,\ z = \sqrt[3]{2}\,(\cos140° + i\sin140°)$

· $n = 2,\ z = \sqrt[3]{2}\,(\cos260° + i\sin260°)$

· $n = 0,\ 1,\ 2$ 일 때의 z를 좌표에 나타내면 다음과 같다.

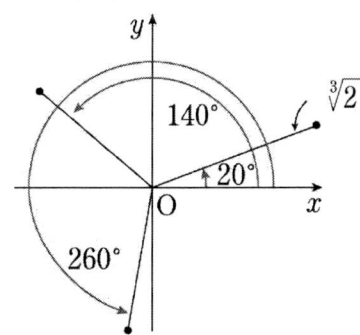

Rotation

다음을 보자.

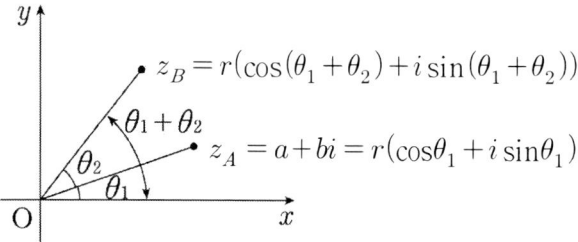

위의 그림에서 Z_A를 θ_2만큼 회전시키면 Z_B가 된다.
자세히 보면 r값은 변하지 않고 θ_1이 $\theta_1 + \theta_2$가 되었다.
그래서 다음과 같이 생각할 수 있다.

$$Z_B = \underbrace{r(\cos\theta_1 + i\sin\theta_1)}_{=(a+bi)} \times \underbrace{1 \cdot (\cos\theta_2 + i\sin\theta_2)}_{=(c+di)}$$
$$= r(\cos(\theta_1 + \theta_2) + i\sin(\theta_1 + \theta_2))$$

즉, 주어진 Complex Number에 $r=1$인 Complex Number를
곱하면 회전한 좌표를 찾을 수 있다.

Trigonometric Form끼리 곱해도 되고 Standard Form끼리
곱해도 되지만 Special Angle이 아닌 이상 Standard Form끼리
곱하는 것이 편할 때가 많다. 여기서 한 가지 분명히 해 둘 것은
원점(Origin)을 중심으로 회전한다는 것이다.

원점(Origin)을 중심으로 회전하지 않는 경우에는 회전
중심을 원점(Origin)으로 이동시켜서 회전을 시켜야 한다.

다음의 예제를 보자.

(Example) Point z_1 created by rotating

Point $\sqrt{3}+i$ about origin point by $90°$

(Solution) 이 문제의 경우 좌표에 그려보면 바로 정답이 $(-1, \sqrt{3})$ 이라는 사실을 알 수 있다. 하지만 모든 문제가 이 문제처럼 간단하지는 않으므로 다음의 풀이를 알아 두도록 하자.

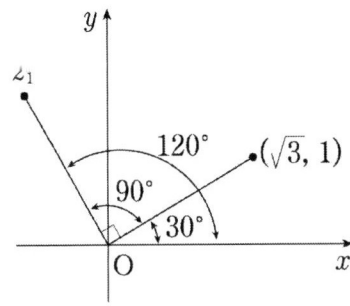

$\Rightarrow$ $\sqrt{3}+i=2(\cos30°+i\sin30°)$이므로 $1 \cdot (\cos90°+i\sin90°)$를 곱하면

$2(\cos30°+i\sin30°) \times 1 \cdot (\cos90°+i\sin90°)=2(\cos120°+i\sin120°)$

$=2(-\dfrac{1}{2}+\dfrac{\sqrt{3}}{2}i)=-1+\sqrt{3}i$ 이므로 $(-1, \sqrt{3})$

앞의 풀이는 Trigonometric Form을 곱해서 구했지만
우리가 모르는 Angle (예를 들어, $\cos20°$, $\sin110°$, $\cdots$)이
나오는 경우가 더 많기 때문에 다음과 같이
Standard Form을 곱하는 방법으로 푸는 것도 알아 두어야 한다.

$$\Rightarrow (\sqrt{3}+i) \times \boxed{1 \cdot (\cos 90° + i \sin 90°)} = i$$
$$= (\sqrt{3}+i) \times i = \sqrt{3}i + i^2 = -1 + \sqrt{3}i$$

(Example) Point z_1 created by rotating

Point $2+i$ about origin point by $120°$

(Solution) $2+i$를 Trigonometric Form 으로 나타내 보자.

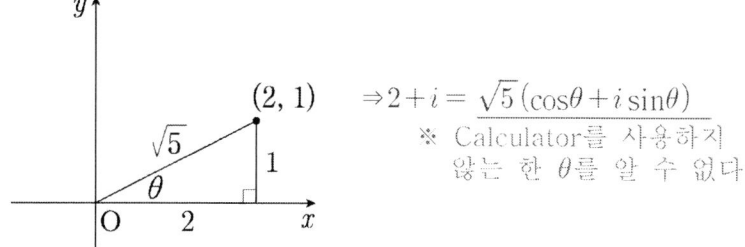

$$\Rightarrow 2+i = \sqrt{5}(\cos\theta + i\sin\theta)$$
※ Calculator를 사용하지
않는 한 θ를 알 수 없다.

이 문제를 Trigonometric Form을 곱하는 방법으로 풀어보자.
$$\sqrt{5}(\cos\theta + i\sin\theta) \times 1 \cdot (\cos 120° + i\sin 120°)$$

$$= \sqrt{5}(\cos(\theta + 120°) + i\sin(\theta + 120°))$$

$\Rightarrow \theta$를 모르기 때문에 z_1을 구할 수 없다.

그래서 Standard Form끼리 곱하는 방법으로 구해본다.

$$\Rightarrow (2, i) \times \underline{1 \cdot (\cos 120° + i\sin 120°)}$$
$$= -\frac{1}{2} + \frac{\sqrt{3}}{2}i$$
$$= (2+i)(-\frac{1}{2} + \frac{\sqrt{3}}{2}i) = -1 + \sqrt{3}i - \frac{1}{2}i - \frac{\sqrt{3}}{2} = -\frac{2+\sqrt{3}}{2} + \frac{\sqrt{3}-1}{2}i$$

그러므로, $(-\frac{2+\sqrt{3}}{2}, \frac{\sqrt{3}-1}{2})$

(Example) Point z created by rotating

Point $2+i$ about $-1+2i$ by $90°$

(Solution)

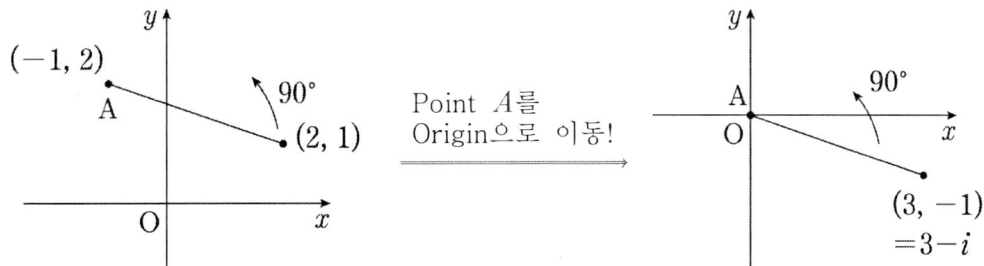

⇒ 즉, $3-i$를 $90°$회전! Standard Form을 곱한다!

$$(3-i) \times \underset{=i}{\underline{\frac{1 \cdot (\cos 90° + i\sin 90°)}{}}}$$

⇒ $(3-i) \cdot i = 1+3i = (1,3)$

$(1, 3)$을 다시 x축으로 -1, y축으로 2만큼
이동시키면 $(0, 5)$가 되므로 $5i$

Conjugate Roots

$z = \alpha + \beta i$의 Conjugate Root는 $\overline{z} = \alpha - \beta i$ 이다.
Conjugate Root는 다음과 같은 성질을 갖는다.

1. Conjugate Root끼리 곱하고 더하면 i가 사라진다.

2. 주어진 Equation의 Coefficient가 Real Number 일 때,
   Equation은 Conjugate Root를 갖는다.

다음을 보자.

① $x^2 + ix + 1 = 0$

$$x_1 = \frac{-i + \sqrt{5}\,i}{2}, \quad x_2 = \frac{-i - \sqrt{5}\,i}{2}$$

여기에서 x_1과 x_2는 Conjugate Root가 아니다.

이유는 $x_1 + x_2 = -i,\ x_1 \cdot x_2 = 1$ 인데

$x_1 + x_2$에서 i가 없어지지 않았기 때문이다.

② $x^2 + x + 1 = 0$

$$x_1 = \frac{-1 + \sqrt{3}\,i}{2} \qquad\qquad x_2 = \frac{-1 - \sqrt{3}\,i}{2}$$

여기에서 $x_1 + x_2 = -1,\ x_1 \cdot x_2 = 1$이므로

$x_1 + x_2,\ x_1 \cdot x_2$ 모두 i가 사라졌다.

그러므로, x_1과 x_2는 Conjugate Root이다.

②번처럼 Equation의 Coefficient가 Real Number 일 때,
Conjugate Root를 갖는다.

246

Property of Complex Number

다음의 Complex Number의 특성은 반드시 암기하여야 한다.

1. $a+bi = c+di$ (a, b, c, d real number)
   $\Leftrightarrow a = c, \ b = d$

2. $z\bar{z} = |z|^2 = |\bar{z}|^2$

(Proof)

$z = 2+i$ 라고 하면 $\bar{z} = 2-i$

· $z\bar{z} = (2+i)(2-i) = 4-i^2 = 5$

· $|z| = \sqrt{2^2+1^2} = \sqrt{5}$ 에서 $|z|^2 = \sqrt{5}^2 = 5$

· $|\bar{z}| = \sqrt{2^2+(-1)^2} = \sqrt{5}$ 에서 $|\bar{z}|^2 = \sqrt{5}^2 = 5$

3. $|z_1 \times z_2| = |z_1| \times |z_2|$

(Proof)

$z_1 = 1+2i \quad z_2 = 2-i$ 라고 하면

$z_1 \times z_2 = (1+2i)(2-i) = 2-i+4i+2 = 4+3i$

그러므로, $|z_1 \times z_2| = \sqrt{4^2+3^2} = 5$.

· $|z_1| = \sqrt{1^2+2^2} = \sqrt{5}$ · $|z_2| = \sqrt{2^2+(-1)^2} = \sqrt{5}$

그러므로, $|z_1| \times |z_2| = 5$

4. $|c \times z| = c \times |z|$

(Proof)

$c = 3, \ z = 1+i$ 라고 하면

· $|c \times z| = \sqrt{3^2+3^2} = \sqrt{18} = 3\sqrt{2}$

· $|z| = \sqrt{1^2+1^2} = \sqrt{2}$ 에서 $3 \times |z| = 3\sqrt{2}$

5. $|z|^n = |z^n|$

(Proof)

$z = 1 + 2i$라고 하면,

· $|z|^2 = \sqrt{1^2 + 2^2}^2 = \sqrt{5}^2 = 5$

· $z^2 = 1 + 4i + 4i = -3 + 4i$ 에서

$|z^2| = \sqrt{(-3)^2 + 4^2} = 5$

6. $|z_1 - z_2|$ 는 평면상에서의 두 점 사이의 거리를 의미한다.

(Proof)

$z_1 = a + bi$, $z_2 = c + di$라고 하면,

$z_1 - z_2 = (a - c) + (b - di)$ 에서

$|z_1 - z_2| = \sqrt{(a-c)^2 + (b-d)^2}$

7. · $\overline{z_1 \pm z_2} = \overline{z_1} \pm \overline{z_2}$　　· $\overline{z_1 \times z_2} = \overline{z_1} \times \overline{z_2}$　　· $\overline{\left(\dfrac{z_1}{z_2}\right)} = \dfrac{\overline{z_1}}{\overline{z_2}}$

8. $\left|\dfrac{z_2}{z_1}\right| = \dfrac{|z_2|}{|z_1|}$

(Proof)

$z_1 = 1 + i$, $z_2 = 2 + i$라고 하면,

· $\left|\dfrac{z_2}{z_1}\right| = \left|\dfrac{(2+i)(1-i)}{(1+i)(1-i)}\right| = \left|\dfrac{3-i}{2}\right| = \dfrac{\sqrt{3^2 + (-1)^2}}{2} = \dfrac{\sqrt{10}}{2}$

· $\dfrac{|z_2|}{|z_1|} = \dfrac{\sqrt{2^2 + 1^2}}{\sqrt{1^2 + 1^2}} = \dfrac{\sqrt{5}}{\sqrt{2}} = \dfrac{\sqrt{10}}{2}$

01. If $i^2 = -1$, then $(i - i^{-1}) =$

(A) 0

(B) $-2i$

(C) $2i$

(D) $-\dfrac{i}{2}$

(E) $\dfrac{i}{2}$

02. If S is the set of points z in the complex plane such that $(3+4i)z$ is a real number, then S is a

(A) right triangle

(B) circle

(C) hyperbola

(D) line

(E) parabola

03. If the six solutions of $x^6 = -64$ are written in the form $a+bi$, where a and b are real, then the product of those solutions with $a > 0$ is

(A) -2

(B) 0

(C) $2i$

(D) 4

(E) 16

04. Let $i = \sqrt{-1}$. Define a sequence of complex numbers by $z_1 = 0$, $z_{n+1} = z_n^2 + i$ for $n \geq 1$. In the complex plane, how far from the origin is z_{111}?

(A) 1

(B) $\sqrt{2}$

(C) $\sqrt{3}$

(D) $\sqrt{110}$

(E) $\sqrt{2^{55}}$

05. Let $i = \sqrt{-1}$. The product of the real parts of the roots of $z^2 - z = 5 - 5i$ is

(A) -25

(B) -6

(C) -5

(D) $\dfrac{1}{4}$

(E) 25

06. The complex number z satisfies $z + |z| = 2 + 8i$. What is $|z|^2$? Note : if $z = a + bi$, then $|z| = \sqrt{a^2 + b^2}$.

(A) 68

(B) 100

(C) 169

(D) 208

(E) 289

250

07. What is the area of triangle on a complex plane that has three complex number that satisfies $z^3 = i$ as its vertices?

(A) $\dfrac{3}{4}$

(B) 1

(C) $\dfrac{3\sqrt{3}}{4}$

(D) 3

(E) $3\sqrt{3}$

08. The polynomial $f(x) = x^4 + ax^3 + bx^2 + cx + d$ has real coefficients, and $f(2i) = f(2+i) = 0$. What is $a+b+c+d$?

(A) 0

(B) 1

(C) 4

(D) 9

(E) 16

09. A polynomial of degree four with leading coefficient 1 and integer coefficients has two zeros, both of which are integers. Which of the following can also be a zero of the polynomial?

(A) $\dfrac{1+i\sqrt{11}}{2}$

(B) $\dfrac{1+i}{2}$

(C) $\dfrac{1}{2}+i$

(D) $1+\dfrac{i}{2}$

(E) $\dfrac{1+i\sqrt{13}}{2}$

10. A function f is defined by $f(z)=i\,\overline{z}$, where $i=\sqrt{-1}$ and $\overline{z}$ is the complex conjugate of z. How many values of z satisfy both $|z|=5$ and $f(z)=z$?

(A) 0

(B) 1

(C) 2

(D) 4

(E) 8

252

11. For complex number z which $|z| = 1$, what is the maximum value of non-real part of $z + iz$?

   (A) 1

   (B) $\sqrt{2}$

   (C) 2

   (D) $\sqrt{5}$

   (E) 3

12. Let S be the sum of all the real coefficients of the expansion of $(1 + ix)^{4015}$. What is S?

   (A) 0

   (B) 1

   (C) 2^{507}

   (D) 2^{2007}

   (E) 2^{4015}

13. Find $\displaystyle\sum_{k=0}^{49}(-1)^k\binom{99}{2k}$, where $\displaystyle\binom{n}{j}=\frac{n!}{j!(n-j)!}$.

(A) -2^{50}

(B) -2^{49}

(C) 0

(D) 2^{49}

(E) 2^{50}

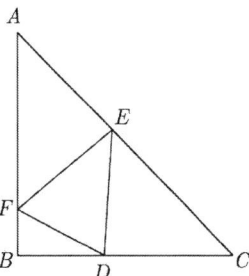

14. The figure above shows a right triangle $\triangle ABC$. The legs $\overline{AB}$ and $\overline{BC}$ each have 4. An equilateral triangle $\triangle DEF$ is inscribed in $\triangle ABC$ as shown. Point D is the midpoint of $\overline{BC}$. What is the length of $\overline{BF}$?

(A) 1

(B) $\sqrt{2}$

(C) $4\sqrt{3}-6$

(D) $4\sqrt{2}$

(E) $4\sqrt{3}+2$

15. The points $(0, 0)$, $(a, 11)$, and $(b, 37)$ are the vertices of an equilateral triangle. What is the value of ab?

   (A) 25
   (B) 135
   (C) 250
   (D) 315
   (E) 420

16. Let $p(x) = x^3 + ax^2 + bx + c$, where a, b, and c are complex numbers. Suppose that $p(2009 + 9002\pi i) = p(2009) = p(9002) = 0$. What is the number of nonreal zeros of $x^{12} + ax^8 + bx^4 + c$?

   (A) 4
   (B) 6
   (C) 8
   (D) 10
   (E) 12

17. The solutions of the equation $z^4 + 4z^3 i - 6z^2 - 4zi - i = 0$ are the vertices of a convex polygon in the complex plane. What is the area of the polygon?

(A) $2^{\frac{5}{8}}$

(B) $2^{\frac{3}{4}}$

(C) 2

(D) $2^{\frac{5}{4}}$

(E) $2^{\frac{3}{2}}$

18. Find the number of ordered pairs of real numbers (a, b) such that $(a + bi)^{2002} = a - bi$.

(A) 1001

(B) 1002

(C) 2001

(D) 2002

(E) 2004

256

19. If z is a complex number such that $z+z^{-1} = \sqrt{3}$, what is the value of $z^{2010} + z^{-2010}$?

(A) -1

(B) -2

(C) -3

(D) 2

(E) 1

20. What is the sum of the roots of $z^{12} = 64$ that have a positive real part?

(A) 2

(B) 4

(C) $\sqrt{2}+2\sqrt{3}$

(D) $2\sqrt{2}+\sqrt{6}$

(E) $(1+\sqrt{3})+(1+\sqrt{3})i$

21. There are 24 different complex numbers z such that $z^{24} = 1$. For how many of these is z^6 a real number?

(A) 0

(B) 4

(C) 6

(D) 12

(E) 24

22. In the figure below, $\triangle ABC$ is an equilateral triangle.

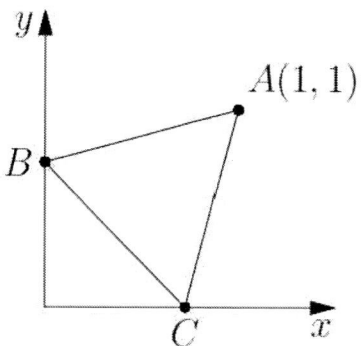

Point A has coordinates $(1, 1)$, point B is on the positive y-axis, and point C is on the positive x-axis. What is the area of $\triangle ABC$?

(A) $2\sqrt{3} - 3$

(B) $2\sqrt{3} - 2$

(C) $2\sqrt{3} - 1$

(D) $2\sqrt{3}$

(E) 4

23. Let z_1, z_2, x_3, and z_4 be the four distinct complex solutions of the equation $z^4 - 6z^2 + 8z + 1 = -4(z^3 - z + 2)i$. What is the sum of the six pairwise distances between z_1, z_2, z_3 and z_4?

(A) $6\sqrt{3} + 2$

(B) $6\sqrt{3} + 3$

(C) $6\sqrt{3} + 4$

(D) $6\sqrt{3} + 5$

(E) $6\sqrt{3} + 6$

24. What is the number of ordered pairs of complex numbers (u, v) such that $uv = 10$ and such that the real and imaginary parts of u and v are integers?

(A) 40

(B) 42

(C) 44

(D) 46

(E) 48

25. Let b_1, b_2, b_3, c_1, c_2, and c_3 be real numbers such that for every real number x, we have $x^6 - x^5 + x^4 - x^3 + x^2 - x + 1 = (x^2 + b_1 x + c_1)(x^2 + b_2 x + c_2)(x^2 + b_3 x + c_3)$. What is the value of $b_1 c_1 + b_2 c_2 + b_3 c_3$?

(A) -1

(B) -2

(C) 0

(D) 1

(E) 2

26. Let $A = (2, 0)$, $B = (0, 2)$, $C = (-2, 0)$, and $D = (0, -2)$. Which of the following the greatest possible value of the product $PA \cdot PB \cdot PC \cdot PD$, where P is a point on the circle $x^2 + y^2 = 9$?

(A) 80

(B) 85

(C) 90

(D) 94

(E) 97

ANSWER KEY

1. Algebra

1. (D)	6. (D)	11. (A)	16. (D)
2. (D)	7. (B)	12. (D)	17. (B)
3. (B)	8. (D)	13. (A)	18. (A)
4. (A)	9. (B)	14. (B)	19. (A)
5. (C)	10. (D)	15. (E)	20. (D)

2. Equation

1. (B)	6. (B)	11. (D)	16. (C)	21. (A)
2. (A)	7. (D)	12. (B)	17. (E)	22. (B)
3. (B)	8. (D)	13. (B)	18. (C)	23. (B)
4. (B)	9. (D)	14. (D)	19. (E)	24. (E)
5. (B)	10. (D)	15. (D)	20. (D)	

3. Integer 1

1. (B)	11. (A)	21. (E)	31. (C)	41. (E)
2. (C)	12. (E)	22. (C)	32. (D)	
3. (A)	13. (B)	23. (D)	33. (B)	
4. (A)	14. (C)	24. (A)	34. (D)	
5. (D)	15. (E)	25. (C)	35. (D)	
6. (D)	16. (E)	26. (A)	36. (B)	
7. (B)	17. (B)	27. (A)	37. (A)	
8. (D)	18. (B)	28. (D)	38. (E)	
9. (B)	19. (E)	29. (E)	39. (D)	
10. (A)	20. (C)	30. (D)	40. (B)	

4. Integer 2

1. (A)	4. (C)	7. (B)	10. $p=7$, $q=3$	13. (E)
2. (C)	5. (C)	8. $p=q=2$	11. (C)	
3. (D)	6. (A)	9. 0	12. (D)	

5. Inequality

1. (D)	3. (C)	5. (D)
2. (D)	4. (B)	6. (A)

7. Sequence & Recurrence Formula

1. (C)	5. (C)	9. (A)	13. (C)
2. (E)	6. (C)	10. (A)	14. (D)
3. (E)	7. (C)	11. (B)	15. (B)
4. (B)	8. (B)	12. (D)	16. (E)

8. Counting & Probability

1. (D)	7. (D)	13. (E)	19. (E)	25. (D)
2. (D)	8. (D)	14. (C)	20. (D)	26. (B)
3. (C)	9. (A)	15. (C)	21. (B)	27. (D)
4. (E)	10. (B)	16. (A)	22. (C)	28. (B)
5. (C)	11. (D)	17. (C)	23. (C)	29. (D)
6. (C)	12. (D)	18. (D)	24. (C)	30. (D)

9. Plane Geometry 1

1. (C)	11. (B)	21. (E)	31. (E)	41. (B)
2. (B)	12. (D)	22. (D)	32. (A)	
3. (D)	13. (D)	23. (C)	33. (B)	
4. (C)	14. (D)	24. (B)	34. (D)	
5. (B)	15. (A)	25. (D)	35. (D)	
6. (B)	16. (D)	26. (D)	36. (A)	
7. (B)	17. (D)	27. (C)	37. (D)	
8. (C)	18. (B)	28. (B)	38. (E)	
9. (B)	19. (C)	29. (C)	39. (A)	
10. (B)	20. (B)	30. (D)	40. (A)	

10. Plane Geometry 2

Exercise

1. (D)	3. (C)	5. (D)	7. (B)	9. (B)
2. (A)	4. (A)	6. (D)	8. (C)	10. (D)

Problem

1. (C)	8. (C)	15. (C)	22. (A)	29. (E)
2. (E)	9. (E)	16. (D)	23. (C)	30. (E)
3. (D)	10. (B)	17. (A)	24. (A)	31. (D)
4. (A)	11. (D)	18. (C)	25. (E)	32. (D)
5. (D)	12. (C)	19. (E)	26. (A)	33. (E)
6. (B)	13. (D)	20. (D)	27. (C)	34. (B)
7. (D)	14. (B)	21. (B)	28. (B)	

11. Plane Geometry 3

Exercise

1. 6.5　　2. $\dfrac{59}{8}$　　3. $\sqrt{110}$　　4. 2

Problem

1. (B)	5. (B)	9. (A)	13. (B)	17. (D)
2. (B)	6. (D)	10. (B)	14. (C)	
3. (B)	7. (D)	11. (A)	15. (D)	
4. (E)	8. (C)	12. (E)	16. (C)	

12. Space Geometry

1. (D)	5. (B)	9. (A)	13. (A)
2. (D)	6. (C)	10. (C)	14. (E)
3. (C)	7. (E)	11. (B)	15. (B)
4. (A)	8. (E)	12. (E)	16. (C)

13. Trigonometry

1. (B)   3. (E)   5. (A)   7. (A)

2. (E)   4. (A)   6. (B)

14. Complex Number

1. (C)   7. (C)   13. (B)   19. (B)   25. (A)

2. (D)   8. (D)   14. (C)   20. (D)   26. (E)

3. (D)   9. (A)   15. (D)   21. (D)

4. (B)   10. (C)   16. (C)   22. (A)

5. (B)   11. (B)   17. (D)   23. (E)

6. (E)   12. (D)   18. (E)   24. (E)

심선생의~
AMC10 AMC12 만점정복

발행일 2017년 11월16일
지은이 심현성
편집 도비출판사 편집부
발행처 도비출판사 발행인 이태구
주소 충남 서산시 읍내동 82-13 2층 전화 1544-4940 팩스 (041)669-1732
홈페이지 www.dbedu.co.kr 등록번호 제 453-2007-00006호